Making Sense of Race, Class, and Gender

Making Sense of Race, Class, and Gender

Commonsense, Power, and Privilege in the United States

CELINE-MARIE PASCALE

Routledge
Taylor & Francis Group
New York London

Routledge is an imprint of the
Taylor & Francis Group, an informa business

Routledge
Taylor & Francis Group
270 Madison Avenue
New York, NY 10016

Routledge
Taylor & Francis Group
2 Park Square
Milton Park, Abingdon
Oxon OX14 4RN

© 2007 by Taylor & Francis Group, LLC
Routledge is an imprint of Taylor & Francis Group, an Informa business

Printed in the United States of America on acid-free paper
10 9 8 7 6 5 4 3 2 1

International Standard Book Number-10: 0-415-95537-8 (Softcover) 0-415-95536-X (Hardcover)
International Standard Book Number-13: 978-0-415-95537-9 (Softcover) 978-0-415-95536-2 (Hardcover)

Library of Congress Cataloging-in-Publication Data

Pascale, Celine-Marie, 1956-
    Making sense of race, class, and gender : commonsense, power, and privilege in the U.S. / Celine-Marie Pascale.
        p. cm.
    Includes bibliographical references and index.
    ISBN 0-415-95536-X (hb) -- ISBN 0-415-95537-8 (pb)
    1. Social perception--United States. 2. Classism--United States. 3. Racism--United States. 4. Sexism--United States. 5. Sexism in language--United States. 6. Racism in language. 7. Social classes in mass media. 8. Commonsense reasoning--United States. 9. Discourse analysis. I. Title.

HN59.2.P383 2007
305.30973--dc22   2006028462

Visit the Taylor & Francis Web site at
http://www.taylorandfrancis.com

and the Routledge Web site at
http://www.routledge-ny.com

CONTENTS

PREFACE

There is a profound irony in my writing a book about commonsense knowledge. As a child absorbed in books, growing up in a family that did not value reading, I was often chastised for overthinking things and missing what others understood as obvious—yet when I entered university, I found myself awash in commonsensical assumptions that others did not share. I recall the first time someone in a university classroom asked: "What does it mean to be middle class?" A dead silence fell. As an earnest but naïve student, I suggested that by virtue of the fact that we were in a college classroom, we were all middle class. The room exploded in fury and when the dust settled, for the first time in my life, I began to wonder about my own class position.

My family always thought of itself as middle class—even during the year that my mother bought groceries for us by selling her blood to blood banks. I was eight years old when my father, who had been a truck salesman, lost his job because of illness. My mother took her first job as a nurse's aide on the graveyard shift of a state psychiatric hospital. She worked hard to support two adults and four children, to "make ends meet," on minimum wage. It frightened us all to see the ends constantly moving further apart. We moved from the creeks and farms of a then small neighborhood to a more urban environment, on the outskirts of a wealthy community with a good school system. I would now sit in classes with kids who went to Europe on summer vacation and I would return home each day to do the cooking and cleaning for our family of six.

Although my mother's paycheck was never enough, we had other resources: a butcher who gave my mother baloney butts and soup bones, a relative in a convent who gave us underwear, and people who passed along clothes. At times, my mother enlisted my help to steal groceries, sacks of potatoes, or flour from the supermarket. She was determined to spare us the hunger she had known as a child. Sheets and towels appeared in the hall closet, all stamped with the state psychiatric hospital name in large blocked letters. Through it all, we never doubted that we were middle class. All of the poor white people I have ever known have thought of themselves as "middle class." Today I may be the only member of my family who would look back and call us working poor. This is one of the many mixed-gifts of my education. Whose language should I use to describe my family? The impossibility of this choice came to inspire my sociological interest in language and meaning.

In profound ways, the second wave of feminism was a lifesaver for me. As the only daughter in a family with four children, I grew up learning to cater to the needs of men. I learned early that my well-being depended on their happiness. Even as a child, I knew that my mother was able to coax the butcher into giving her baloney butts and soup bones because she was a woman. And, I knew that being a woman made it impossible for her to get credit, even long after my father had died. Because I was a girl, I was spared the regular and near-deadly violence of my father's rage. I was spared the need to prove myself, as my brothers did, in knife-fights and various forms of daring crime. And because I was a girl, I was the frequent target of sexual abuse. Feminism gave me a framework for understanding my experiences as a young woman and for exploring my sexuality. I came out as a lesbian for the first time in 1977; it took almost 20 more years for me come out as a bisexual. Being bisexual, and having a lifetime commitment to a woman, has unsettled many familial and community relationships. The lesbian feminist movement of the late 1970s opened many new horizons, even as it was troubled by its own extensions of privilege—most especially with respect to sexuality, class, and whiteness.

Race privilege was central to shaping both my family's history and its future. The civil rights movement reverberated through my childhood as a force my family protected me from. As a small child, I understood being surrounded by white people as simply "normal." I never saw the public expressions of racism that must have existed in order to maintain segregation. My oldest brother consistently resisted racism and made a space for me to do so as well. Yet while I was sure that racism was wrong, I was equally sure that "all people were the same." For years after leaving home, I continued to be most comfortable in white communities, even as I argued against racism. My best intentions sadly exceeded my best abilities. In the second wave of feminism, I was among the many white women who needed to learn to negotiate the relationship between my gender oppression and my race privilege. I have learned to appreciate that building an understanding of and commitment to racial justice is a life-long process that both honors and accrues many debts.

The legacies of the women's liberation movement, the civil rights movement, the American Indian movement, and the Stonewall riots, have been profound. And yet all movements for social justice are limited by their own time and place; even though their momentum once propelled a new future, their logic and methods cannot serve as the logic and method of contemporary movements for social change. Every era must, in some way, create its own means. This book is an effort to rethink some categories of difference that have formed the basis of social justice organizing in the past, in the hopes of contributing to new ways of thinking about social justice and social justice movements in the present.

Today I am among the first generation in my family to hold a high school degree, and the only member of my family to attend a university. For most people in my family, education is not a marker of success, and my mentioning it here is not intended to separate my life from theirs as a story of success. Rather, I understand my life as a paradox of class migration, in which an arduous journey brings me to a place where I can never fully arrive. My life in transit is separate yet entwined, impossibly connected and alien. In this sense, my research connects me to my past, even as it seemingly carries me away toward a different future.

This is one narrative of a history that situates me in relationship to the people I interviewed, the media I studied, and the book I have written. It is a history that also profoundly shaped my relationship to sociology. Despite the many changes the 1960s and 1970s brought to sociology, a lot of what I learned in graduate study failed to speak to the experiences of the people I have known. So it was more from alienation than hubris (although they are related here) that I began to reconsider sociological knowledge about race, class, and gender and to weigh the political commitments of sociological theory and methods. It was important to me to understand how people make race, class, and gender meaningful in their daily lives, while also considering the relations of power that shape both daily experiences and the local productions of meaning. My interests led me to craft a style of discourse analysis inflected by the interpretative frameworks of ethnomethodology and poststructural discourse analysis. The method is as sociological as the analysis is heterodox.

I want to thank the editorial staff at Routledge for their unwavering support for this book in particular, and for their sustained support for interdisciplinary studies of language more generally. I owe many thanks to Judith Simon for skillfully managing the transformation of manuscript pages into a bound book. This book is an elaboration of research I conducted for my dissertation. As might be clear, I was not a traditional graduate student and owe a great deal of thanks to all of the faculty, staff, and graduate students in the Department of Sociology at the University of California, Santa Cruz, for the formal and informal mentoring that helped me to develop the habits of a scholar, without losing my heart, my dreams, or my edges. I most especially thank John Brown Childs and Melanie Dupuis for providing buoyancy in my intellectual life.

It is impossible to overstate the importance of mentors who have helped so much to shape this work—and equally impossible to find adequate words. I owe a profound and very special debt to Bettina Aptheker, Herman Gray, Joseph Schneider, and Candace West for their patience, wisdom, and generosity. I offer special thanks to colleagues Melanie Heath, Kelly Joyce, John Kelly, Laura Mamo, and Salvador Vidal-Ortiz for their thoughtful comments and insights on various drafts. In addition, for their advice and encouragement on early incarnations of this work I thank Lyle Blake, Marilyn Chap, Valerie Chase, Don Fong, Marie Garcia, Linda Hemby, Akasha Hull, Helen Resnick-Sannes, Bobbie Reyes, Cynthia Siemsen, Valerie Simmons, Lin Soriano, Deborah Turner, David Watson, and Carol Whitehill. And, without question, my own graduate students, especially those in Multiculturalism and the Sociology of Language, have profoundly helped me to refine my thinking. This book would look quite different without their weekly contributions to issues of identity, equality, and language. I am sure any success this book might have will be due to the many readers' comments that have helped to refine my thinking. Of course, whatever limitations remain are entirely my own. I hope that the shortcomings, as well as the successes, of this book will contribute to productive discussions and useful insights that help to advance sociological understandings of language, culture, and power.

The work required for this book would have been impossible without the love and support of friends and family, especially Larry Bernstien, Judith Cohen, David Pascale, Dorothy and Manuel Santos, and Tasha Turzo. Most especially, I thank my spouse, Mercedes Teresa Santos for her thoughtful reading of many drafts of this book and for her remarkable wisdom and humor. I close with deep gratitude for Ven. Segyu Choepel Rinpoche, Christina Juskiewicz, Breck Caloss, Taria Joy, Susan Krafft, Pam Moriarity, and Jeanne Vaughn.

1

INTRODUCTION

The aspects of things that are most important for us are hidden because of their simplicity and familiarity. (One is unable to notice something—because it is always before one's eyes.) The real foundations of his enquiry do not strike a man [sic] at all. Unless that fact has at some time struck him.—And this means: we fail to be struck by what, once seen, is most striking and most powerful. (Wittgenstein 1951, 50)

The universe is made of stories, not atoms. (Muriel Rukeyser, quoted in *Write to the Heart*)

In the United States, the twenty-first century opened with white women and people of color still struggling for adequate health care, reproductive rights, and equal wages, as well as for access to employment and education. Racial profiling is still considered "good policy," and more frequently, a matter of national security. Recent legislation and sentencing procedures have produced the largest per capita prison population in the world—as well as unprecedented government-sponsored surveillance, disappearances (aka renditions), and torture. At the same time, the federal government has reduced funding for welfare, public education, public broadcasting, and arts. Everyday the nation enjoys an abundance of food, but the workers who harvest the fields and orchards still labor under the enormous risks of pesticide poisoning. In some cases, migrant farm workers live in conditions of slavery and in other cases they earn wages as low as $50 for every 4,000 pounds of produce picked (Nieves 2005). Millions of adults and children, unable to afford housing, live in cardboard shelters on side-walks, in doorways, and under freeways.

While gains in civil rights have been considerable, those gains surely are both incomplete and under erosion. Both inside and outside of the academy, the need for progressive politics is evident; however, less clear is the adequacy of the original civil rights vision to deal with contemporary issues of inequality (cf., Omi 1996). In the United States, capacities for social justice organizing remain tenuously anchored to the class-based analyses of the (largely white male) political left and the "identity-based" politics of people of color, feminists, and lesbian, gay, bisexual, and transgender (LGBT) movements. Clearly, all marginalized people are in need of more effective organizing strategies. This book takes as its premise that how we negotiate the challenges of inequal-ity in the twenty-first century depends less on what we consciously *think* about "difference" and more on what we inadvertently *assume*. By examining practices that reveal commonsense knowledge, this book makes a unique contribution that demonstrates how race, gender, and class are made visible and meaningful as apparently routine matters of social difference. My analysis illustrates how commonsense knowledge can sustain systems of inequality without mobilizing conscious feelings of bigotry or prejudice. Further, I examine how commonsense functions to naturalize historical relations of power and privilege. Throughout, I consider how local practices, and the discourses that shape local prac-tices, are analytically, pragmatically, and politically linked.[1] I retheo-rize race, gender, and class and explore corresponding implications and strategies for social change.

In addition, an overarching goal of this book is to produce a fuller understanding of the productive force of language with respect to race, gender, and class. I draw from both ethnomethodology and post-structural discourse analysis to analyze the production of common-sense knowledge at local and cultural levels. Ethnomethodology is an interpretative paradigm that examines local contexts to understand how people cooperatively engage in practices that produce a sense of a shared, objective social world.[2] As such, it provides important tools for examining local practices that constitute race, gender, and class. However, precisely because ethnomethodological analyses are not intended to address the broader cultural contexts that inform interac-tion, they often create the appearance that each person is an entirely autonomous subject—free to speak or act in accord with her or his own free will within the confines of a local context. Therefore, I draw from poststructural discourse analysis to situate an understanding of local practices within broader cultural discourses. The analytical interest for poststructural discourse analysis does not regard what one says, but rather, what constitutes the domain of the sayable from within which one is able to speak—hence the characteristic concern with issues of power and culture. Poststructuralist analyses (cf., Butler 1990; 1997a, 1997b; Derrida 1976, 1982; Foucault 1977, 1978, 1980) examine the conditions of knowledge from within which meaning is constructed.

Foucault's (1978) and Butler's (1990, 1993) concern with the social processes that produce and naturalize sex, gender, and sexuality nearly inverts the sense of agency central to ethnomethodology. Yet, despite an emphasis on discursive *practices*, poststructural analyses of the historical and cultural processes of discursive formations can create the appearance that daily interactions are functionally overdetermined.[3] If all of social thought and interaction is determined by the limits of a preexisting language, it becomes impossible to understand resistance and change as anything but accidental. Hence, and one can see why ethnomethodology might provide important and complementary tools for analysis.

Poststructural discourse analysis and ethnomethodology, each working at different levels of analysis, provide analytical resources for understanding race, class, and gender as activities or processes. Both are premised on epistemologies that regard language as a constitutive force that produces social realities, rather than as a transparent vehicle for communication. Broadly speaking, both ethnomethodology and poststructural discourse analysis decenter the subject—that is, they conceptualize subjects as constituted, rather than as preexisting, stable entities. And, both deny an empirical epistemology in which the meaning of a cultural text simply has to be read, in order to be understood. Ethnomethodology exposes the practical reasoning subsumed in everyday practices, while poststructural discourse analysis reveals the cultural processes through which this reasoning is invented and subsumed. This book does not synthesize the fields of ethnomethodology and poststructural discourse analysis but draws tools from each paradigm to produce a fuller understanding of local practices and cultural processes. It is the first book to draw from both ethnomethodology and poststructural discourse analysis to analyze empirical data. And, as such, it demonstrates a potentially powerful means for understanding race, gender, and class in new ways.

Subsequent sections in this chapter introduce readers to a sociological understanding of commonsense knowledge as well as to a broad overview of epistemological divisions in scholarship regarding race, gender, and class. To orient readers to the underlying ethnomethodological and poststructural aspects of this book, I have included a final section that sketches critical aspects of each of the interpretative frameworks that inflect this analysis. In addition, I provide a brief explanation of why this particular analytical framework is useful, given the numbers of other existing ways to analyze language. This section also seeks to clarify potential confusions between this style of analysis and that of related fields. The chapter concludes with an overview of the book.

Commonsense: A Vernacular Morality

Commonsense knowledge is a saturation of cultural knowledge that we cannot fail to recognize and which, through its very obviousness, passes without notice. To the extent that notions of commonsense rest on shared cultural resources, they are able to pass unnoticed in interaction. For instance, a fifteenth-century manual on manners cautions: "It is unseemly to blow your nose in the tablecloth" (Elias 1978, cited in Pollner 1987). Such admonitions are no longer necessary, precisely because they have become a matter of commonsense. A hallmark of commonsense is the belief that the world exists precisely as it is seen; if someone could stand where I am, they would see things the same way as I do.[4] Further, by excluding some topics from consideration, while making others appear obvious, commonsense prepares one to think about the world in particular ways (Handel 1982, 56).

The finite simplicity of commonsense presents the world as self-evident and familiar by reducing the availability of information that would present contradictions, ambiguities, or complications. To the commonsense view, the world appears to be finite and familiar—something that everyone can and should recognize (Geertz 1983). Since there is no motivation to investigate what you already know, "the ontological assumptions of commonsense protect it from scrutiny" (Handel 1982, 56). The knowledge of commonsense is not open to debate, persuasion, or compromise; it has no need of authorities because things simply are what they are.

What sets commonsense knowledge apart from other forms of knowledge is its extraordinary power to eclipse competing accounts of reality; and, in this way, commonsense knowledge functions as a forceful vernacular morality. The moral authority of commonsense lies in its ability to marginalize other ways of knowing more completely, precisely because it is taken by everyone to be beyond dispute (Miller 1993, 361). In contrast to other forms of knowledge, commonsense is more thoroughly naturalized.

Through commonsense we recognize who "looks" familiar—who belongs and who does not. Morality has long been a tool for recognizing "people like us," and a basis for treating people "not like us" differently.[5] Commonsense functions as a vernacular morality through unreflexive daily practices that reinforce the value people place on their own lives and the lives of others (Schneider 1984; Spector 1987). As such, the sense of normalcy that underpins community is, in part, a product of commonsense knowledge.

Within sociology, the study of moral and ethical values developed along functionalist lines concerned with understanding social decay and social cohesion beginning with Durkheim and Weber and continuing through Parsons.[6] The functionalist roots of morality made it a good fit for early studies of deviance, which developed in American sociology.[7] By contrast, Frankfurt School theorists Horkheimer and Habermas developed a more radically critical analysis of the production of morality. For instance, Horkheimer (1933) argues that morality is a product of bourgeois society; moral values and education are needed precisely because "the common good" contradicts the immediate interests of most people.[8] Habermas departed from the more characteristic Frankfurt School analyses to draw from Kohlberg's psychological stages to argue that morality is not an imposition of alien standards on individuals but inheres in the structure of language—normative validity claims are dependent on a communicatively achieved consensus (Habermas 1993).

The premise of this book is that commonsense knowledge about race, class, and gender is both moral and ideological; it is always the hegemonic effect of power that masks the very relations domination that it articulates. Ideological hegemony operates in the assumptions that we make about life and the things we accept as natural.[9] "'Look, you can see for yourself how things are!' 'Let the facts speak for themselves' is perhaps the arch-statement of ideology—the point being, precisely, that facts *never* 'speak for themselves' but are always *made to speak* by a network of discursive devices" (Zizek 1994, 11). Relations of power become naturalized through commonsense.[10] This is precisely why it is important to examine the commonsense knowledge that allows us to believe that we simply see (or simply fail to see) the presence of gender, race, and class. The "difference" that commonsense leads one to recognize is not just the opposite of sameness; there are far more differences among people that pass unnoticed or without consequence. "Difference" is always a relationship—not a characteristic—shaped by histories of force, exploitation, and domination. These historical relationships are submerged beneath the apparently simple, commonsense recognitions of race, gender, and class.

To understand the production of commonsense knowledge in talk and representation, we do not need to know what is actually "true,"— what "really" is the case—we need only to know what is *accountable* as true (Handel 1982, 39). Consider, for instance, that in the United States, people commonly say "the sun rises," "the sun travels across the sky," and "the sun sets"—even though we *know* the sun does not move. In the sixteenth century Copernicus proved Ptolemy's theory of the universe, developed in the second century, to be false. In the twenty-first century, our *knowledge* is Copernican—that is we *know* the earth rotates on its axis and the sun remains stationary—yet our language is still Ptolemaic. Almost five hundred years after Copernicus, people still talk as if the sun turns and the earth remains stationary.[11] Even astronomers talk about the sun rising and setting. It is not just that we have learned to see the sun move—very violent political, religious, and scientific struggles are submerged in what passes for commonsense in talk about sunrises and sunsets. Knowledge is always a series of struggles (Foucault 1994); language sustains the gaps between knowledge and perception. If we have yet to reconcile a Ptolemaic language with a Copernican reality, how might commonsense knowledge inform talk about, and representations of, race, gender, and class?

Race, Gender, and Class

Scholars have been writing about the social construction of race at least as far back as Frederick Douglas, Ida B. Wells, and W.E.B. Du Bois. The literature on race today is rich with cross currents. Racial formation theory (Omi and Winant 1994) offers a comprehensive analysis of the systematic and simultaneous production of the historical social, legal, political, and economic processes that produced racialized subjects in the United States. Many scholars (cf., Almaguer 1974, 1994; Fields 1983, 1990; Glenn 1985, 2002; Jones 1985; Lowe 1996; Roediger 1991, 1994; Saxton 1971, 1990; Wellman 1993) have elaborated on the historical construction of race during a variety of periods. In addition, critical race theory (cf., Crenshaw 1991, 1995; Delgado 1982, 1995, 1998; Lopez 1996, Matsuda 1989, 1993) provides important insights into both racialization and hate speech through analyses of court rulings. Other scholars analyze the social construction of race and related inequalities (cf., Carby 1987, 1997; Collins 1993; Davis 1983; Gilroy 1993, 2000; Kelley 1994; Lubiano 1992, 1997a, b). Additionally, a field of critical white studies turned the analytical lens from systems of oppression to material analyses of privilege (cf., Blee 1991; Frankenberg 1993, 1997a, b; Ignatiev 1995; Lipsitz 1998; Lopez 1996; Perry 2004; Roediger 1991, 1994, 2002).

It would be fair to say that although each analytical approach is different, historical, legal, and social constructionist analyses share an epistemological continuity that is grounded in the materiality of lived experience. More recently, the epistemological presumption that we can know the world through our lived experience has been troubled by poststructural analyses which critique the "evidence of experience" by arguing that all experience is itself already an interpretation (Scott 1988, 1991). Poststructural analyses refocus understandings of race as an effect of discursive processes, cultural texts, and constitutive performances (cf., Appiah 1985; Chabram-Dernersesian 1997; Dei 2004; Denzin 2001; Fregoso and Chabram 1994; Hall 1993, 1997a, b, c, d, e; Johnson 2003; Kincheloe 1998; Wright 2004). The analytical aim of poststructural discourse analyses is to interrogate cultural knowledge that regulates identity and subjectivity (see Hall 1997c, 6).

Much has been written about the various ways that race is socially produced—yet by and large, people still believe they can see race just by looking. Some scholars argue that we need to eliminate race from the public imagination (cf., Gilroy 2000) while others argue that "whiteness" must be more visibly, and differently, inserted into public notions of race (cf., Lipsitz 1998; Omi and Winant 1994). This book contributes to academic debates about race by locating and deconstructing cultural assumptions in daily practices that make race both apparently self-evident and inherently meaningful.

The commonsensical presence of gender, like that of race, seems at times impervious to new knowledge. Stoller (1968) is often credited with making the distinction between gender, as culturally constructed masculinity/femininity, and sex, as a biological attribute. This distinction forms an enduring legacy that underpins analytically rich fields of materialist feminist analyses (cf., Aptheker 1982, 1989; Bordo 1993, 1999; Ferree 1996; Moraga 1983), standpoint feminism (cf., Hartsock 1987; Collins 1993), and postcolonial feminisms (cf., McClintock 1995; Mohanty 1985). More recently, the notions of gender, which once shaped the women's liberation movement and feminist scholarship, have become troubled. The de-centering effects of postmodernity challenge distinctions between sex and gender through critiques of the "naturalness" of sex and sexuality (Fuss 1989, 1991; Sedgwick 1990) and more broadly challenge notions of reified gendered subjects through theories of performativity (Bell 1999; Butler 1990, 1993, 1995, 1997b; Minh-ha 1989, 1997). However, despite this rich intellectual ground of research and debate, to a commonsense view, gender still appears to be simply the nature of persons.

Further, at a time of unprecedented gaps between rich and poor, the presence and meaning of class in daily life is arguably more vague than at any other time in history. Historically, scholars examined class formation by focusing on the ownership of the means of production (Marx 1978, 1990) and various forms of property (Weber 1978). Neo-Marxists (Poulantzas 1975, 1982; Przeworski 1985; Wright 1989, 1997) have addressed the presence of a middle class and nonmanual wage-laborers. Some scholars have attempted to extend Marx's analysis to account for racialized divisions among workers (Bonacich 1972, Cox 1959, Du Bois 1995, Gordon et al. 1982). Feminist theorists (Acker 1973; Bruegel 1979; Eisenstein 1990; Garnsey 1982; Hartmann 1982; Mitchell 1990) have examined the economic function of women as a reserve labor pool. Yet some feminist scholars (Mies 1986; Bannerji 1995; Guillaumin 1995) have challenged the meaning of productive labor and relations of appropriation while others (Collins 1993; Dill 1992; Glenn 1985) have explored class as one element in a three-part system of interlocking oppression. Moreover, Bourdieu (1996) examined the production of class through cultural forms and developed an analysis of "cultural capital." This analytical shift from economic to cultural capital was a substantial change in conceptualizations of class processes; however, the cultural turn brought even more profound epistemological challenges to historical conceptions of class as scholars (cf., Bettie 2003; Gibson-Graham 1999, 2001; Min 1999; Min and Whang 1999) began to develop class analyses premised on discourse analysis and performativity. While the cultural turn in the social sciences moved academic debates about the significance of gender, race, and class toward increasingly problematized notions of subjectivity, in daily life the apparent obviousness imposed by commonsense continues to drive both talk and behavior in a completely different direction.

This book explores how expressions of commonsense knowledge about race, gender, and class implicitly (re)produce knowledge and power in particular ways. Since the coordinates of power are always produced through knowledge, I follow Foucault's lead and refer to power/knowledge or knowledge/power throughout. I attempt to demonstrate how personal agency, experienced in local contexts, is connected to broader cultural discourses that shape and constrain local possibilities. In short, I hope to demonstrate how social contexts come to inhere in language and how such contexts can be reproduced and challenged in local interaction. Here, and throughout the book, I use "language" to refer to broadly construed systems of representation that include talk, texts, images, etc. Hence, I draw analytical distinctions between talk, discourse, and language.

A Sociological Analysis of Language

The data collection for this book is based on the logic and method of analytic induction that is typically used in qualitative research; however, the analysis is inflected by the interpretative paradigms ethnomethodology and poststructural discourse analysis.[12] While most of sociology regards language as a conduit that provides descriptions of phenomena to be studied, ethnomethodology regards language and interaction as objects of study in their own right. Ethnomethodology is the study of "commonsense knowledge, and the range of procedures and considerations, by means of which the ordinary members of society make sense of, find their way about in, and act on the circumstances in which they find themselves" (Heritage 1984, 4). Hence, ethnomethodology is a radical departure, both in analytical focus and style, from mainstream sociology that "orients to rules, norms, and shared meanings as exogenous explanations" (Holstein and Gubrium 2005, 486). According to the historian of science, Thomas Kuhn (1970, 5) in "normal science," the analytical paradigm that organizes scientific knowledge is itself taken-for-granted; it is the reality from which science proceeds with the puzzle-solving activities of research. Transformations in science arise as researchers come to see paradigms not as truths but as constructs that dominate science at particular times and places in history. And, it is in this sense, that British discourse analysis in U.K. sociology and ethnomethodology and conversation analysis in U.S. sociology have been radical paradigmatic departures in the discipline (see Holstein and Gubrium 2005; Wooffitt 2005).[13]

Within U.S. sociology, analyses of texts and talk generally take the form of conversation analysis and are focused on a highly technical analysis of the sense-making practices that inform the turn-by-turn management of interaction.[14] In the United States, studies of the processes through which *meaning* is produced, frequently are regarded as something other than scientific because there is no claim to something objectively "real" that can be measured. Hence, U.S. sociologists seldom pursue analyses of meaning or language (Long 1997). However, the world can only be known through language, and hence it is language, broadly construed, that organizes knowledge/power. Consequently, I draw from ethnomethodology's broadly interpretative stance to get at the production and circulation of knowledge/power, rather than from the highly technical, or linguistically-oriented, tools of conversation analysis and sociolinguisitics.

Ethnomethodology

There are several strands of ethnomethodology (Atkinson 1988; Maynard and Clayman 1991); some ethnomethodological analyses are linguistically focused, others examine language in a more general context of meaning. Among ethnomethodologists, there are disagreements regarding the value and place of these approaches (Douglas 1970, 33–35). The analytical focus of this book follows an ethnomethodological style of analysis that attends to the *unspoken* knowledge upon which interviewees and media reflexively rely in order to produce the appearance of an apparently objective social world. The object of inquiry is an embedded set of assumptions regarding the nature of objects and events.[15] In such an analysis, rationality and understanding, are the *outcome*s of what people do, not the premises (Sharrock and Anderson 1986).

The analytical emphasis on meaning-making practices relieves any burden of assessing the relative accuracy of descriptions and characterizations. Ethnomethodological analyses are rooted to an ontology that refuses any notion of an *objective* reality by which truth or error might be measured (Pollner 1987). Rather, ethnomethodological analyses investigate how people make sense of the world by examining the interpretive work that people do on a daily basis—the practices through which people accomplish, manage, and sustain, what comes to appear as social facts (Sharrock and Anderson 1986). While Garfinkel rejected the notion of persons as "cultural dopes," who suffer from a false consciousness, he also rejected the premise that "social facts" are consciously accomplished by sovereign subjects; consequently, his analyses focused on describing the "overtly material techniques" of such accomplishments (McHoul and Grace 1993). In order to examine the techniques through which an apparently objective social world is produced, it is essential to suspend notions of a shared culture. For example, Garfinkel's (1967) famous study of Agnes, examined the interactional accomplishments that enabled a biological male to be recognizable to others as a woman.[16]

In particular, my research is informed by the ethnomethodological "documentary method" of analysis. This interpretative practice is quite different from standard analytic induction and other forms of discourse analysis that use observations as a kind of evidence about the world. The documentary method consists of treating appearances as "documents" that point to underlying patterns that are unspoken, yet essential to the production of shared understanding (Garfinkel 1967, 77–79). The appearances and the underlying patterns are reflexively related.

In daily life, people rarely say literally what they mean—some things must pass without saying. The point of documentary analysis is to examine the tacit knowledge underlying what is said that enables what is said to make sense. For example, when someone says "no gifts" the meaning of this statement is produced through more than just these words. The meaning of this statement is also is a product of contextual knowledge that is understood but not remarked upon. How sincere is the expression? Does it apply to all participants? Should it be taken literally? Does the person intend for people to give money instead of gifts? It is impossible to say without having the context. The local or immediate context of the interaction foregrounds and activates "pertinent knowledge and skills and ... provide[s] the situated sense and relevance of activities, then and there" (Zimmerman 1992, 36). The tacit knowledge that people must rely upon to make sense of this statement would become recognizable through the interactional exchange.

In addition, I make use of ethnomethodological notions of accounts and accountability.[17] While people commonly use the word "account" as synonymous with the word "description" (e.g., to give an account of what happened), in ethnomethodological analyses, accounts do much more than describe. Accounts organize and constitute that which they describe. Therefore, accounts might be better understood as adumbrations, or glosses, that point beyond the explicit particulars to "a mass of unstated assumptions" (Heritage 1984, 181). Accounts have two primary functions. First, accounts serve as frameworks through which participants construct what is "real." Second, because accounts construct "the real" they also provide corresponding ways to credit or discredit claims and behavior based on what is apparently real. All accounts depend on the local context for meaning. Through the local context we learn what behaviors are potentially account-able.[18] Within ethnomethodology, the context-dependent nature of accounts is referred to as their indexicality.

As far as possible, I engaged in the ethnomethodological practice of "analytical bracketing," in order to understand everyday "realities" as products and resources. I consistently attempted to adopt an attitude of "ethnomethodological indifference" that compels one to abstain from all judgments about the adequacy, value, and importance of members' accounts (see Garfinkel and Sacks 1970). Of course, such goals are necessarily compromised because one is always implicated in the production of the material to be analyzed as well as in the analysis itself.[19] The question, of course, is one of degree. Unable to escape such limitations, it becomes necessary to weigh the messy incompleteness of such efforts against the insights that such attempts can produce. There is no utopian place to stand outside of presuppositions that form common-sense knowledge; and in this sense, the text is always caught within the dilemma of its own premise, unable to fully escape the weight of its own commonsense knowledge. To varying degrees, such troubles accompany all research and await the critical insights of readers.

Poststructural Discourse Analysis

Like ethnomethodology, poststructural discourse analysis does not purport to offer a description of phenomenon "as they are" but rather as they have been produced. However each works at different levels of analysis. If ethnomethodology's notorious focus on empirical phenomena leads critics to charge it with empiricism, critics of poststructuralism have policed the boundaries of textual analysis through charges of analytical relativism where "anything goes." And in this sense, drawing tools from each paradigm may seem to be an unhappy occasion to all concerned. Yet by challenging the social scientific notion of the borders between local contexts and cultural discourses, I attempt to revise and broaden the notion of a meaningful analytic context. I draw from poststructural discourse analysis to situate the meanings produced in local contexts within a broader cultural context that is ontologically consistent, yet epistemologically distinct. In particular, I use Butler's concept of performativity understood, not a single or deliberate act, but as the process through which discourse produces the effect that it names (Butler 1993, 2). A performative "works" to the extent that it *draws on and covers over* the constitutive conventions by which it was mobilized (Butler 1990, 25)—that is to the extent that it appears to be natural.

I also draw from Foucault's concepts of genealogy and discourse to examine the cultural/historical knowledge that comprises tacit knowledge in local practices. Broadly speaking, a genealogical analysis attempts to identify how relations of power constitute domains of subjects and objects. A genealogical analysis concerns how discourses enable and constrain the conditions that constitute the sayable; it traces the production and circulation of knowledge/power, through which discourses constitute the subject positions that persons come to inhabit (Foucault 1970, 1977, 1978; Butler 1997a,c, 1999). And in this sense, genealogy is useful in coming to understand bodies as the products of particular histories. Poststructural discourse analysis situates meaning in historical contexts and links it to power. From this analytical perspective, analyses of local contexts, which are the basis of ethnomethodology, become problematic. The historicity of language does not occur in a context that can be defined easily by spatial and temporal boundaries. Talk in local contexts always exceeds the circumstances of its production both because it is produced through a preexisting language and because it travels forward in time through repetitions (Butler 1997a). Poststructuralists would argue that by placing spatial and temporal limits on the context of talk to be analyzed, researchers make people appear to be sovereign speakers, free of history. Consequently, a genealogical analysis regards the production and circulation of discourses.

Discursive practices produce characteristic ways of *seeing* by drawing boundaries that define what we see and fail to see, what we accept and contest (Patai 1991). Smith (1999) aptly called discourses "canons of relevance and validity." For these reasons, a study of discourses provides important resources for understanding tacit knowledge in relation to the production of cultural knowledge/power. A study of discourse emphasizes systems of representation that shape the potential meanings in any communication as well as limits, boundaries, instabilities, and negotiations.

Discourses transcend individual formulations because they demarcate the perspectives and standards used to elaborate concepts, theories, and knowledge (Foucault 1972, 1994). An object must be constituted through the historical conditions of discourse in order for anyone to "say anything" about it (Foucault 1972). For example, in Chapter 5, I explore historical, cultural, and geographical specificities that made it possible in the United States to speak about "homelessness."

Because consciousness is a social-ideological fact (Volosinov 1973), the logic of consciousness is the logic of discourse. Even the experience of hunger has discursive or ideological structuring. The bodily sensation of hunger may be experienced in a great variety of ways because hunger is linked (through an array of corresponding words, ideas, images, and practices) to personal, historical, and cultural circumstances. Some examples include the hunger for someone going to a fashionably late dinner at an expensive restaurant, the hunger of a person living on the street who is searching through dumpsters, the hunger of someone with anorexia, the hunger of a group of peasants, or a regiment of soldiers. Hence one quickly comes to see how even the immediacy of physical hunger is understood through a discursive context. All discourse is fundamentally political because discourse advances a particular version of reality, which is used both for further inference and for action.

Why Something New?

Many excellent paradigms currently exist for studying language and warrant some mention here. In addition to British discourse analysis, ethnomethodology, conversation analysis, and poststructural discourse analysis, language is also examined through critical discourse analysis, rhetorical psychology, semiotics, socio-linguistics, social psychology, and speech act theory. Within and across each analytical framework it is relatively easy to find both overlapping as well as contradictory ways of approaching the study of language and interaction. This situation is complicated further by a shared nomenclature that often obscures conflicting meanings and epistemologies. For instance, it would be both accurate and misleading to say that each of these analytical frameworks concerns "discourse." In critical discourse analysis (CDA), the word "discourse" frequently refers to a formal linguistic system that regards social competencies formed through conditions or rules that shape expressions. Whereas for sociologists, "discourse" generally refers more broadly to language use, although it also frequently refers to language use in conversation; and in poststructural discourse analysis (also called French discourse analysis and Foucauldian discourse analysis), "discourse" refers to an epistemological system through which subjects and objects are brought into being. While the analytical terms used by British discourse analysis and CDA appear to have much in common with poststructural discourse analysis, the differences among the ways in which the terms are deployed reflect different epistemologies and analytical foci, as well as different conceptions of agency and subjectivity.[20]

Intellectually, I am compelled by the analytical power that can be derived by strategically drawing from ethnomethodology and poststructural discourse analysis. As distinct levels of analysis, each employs distinct nomenclature; yet at deeper levels of ontology/epistemology they can function as complementary. For example, each regards language as a constitutive force that produces social realities, rather than as a transparent vehicle for communication. Neither posits the presence of an external objective reality to which characterizations might be measured or compared for accuracy. Both ethnomethodology and poststructural discourse analysis attempt to understand the social contingencies through which experience comes to be produced and known as it is—and, each refuses the reification of an objective social world. And, ethnomethodology and poststructural discourse analysis have very useful differences. Where ethnomethodology examines how people assemble meaning from the cultural particulars of situated interaction, discourse analysis is deconstructive, disrupting social conventions by revealing how dominant knowledge and ideas shape daily life. When ethnomethodologists write about commonsense knowledge, they refer both to a technical know-how and to the production of meaning in a local context. Whereas when Foucault writes of knowledge, he refers to the social, historical, and political conditions through which subjects and objects are produced. In immediate social situations, participants in talk determine the *utterances*, but more sustained and basic social connections determine these deeper layers of language (Volosinov 1973).

If individuals exert maximum agency through talk, we exert least in language. Each of us inherits a ready-made language and the words we use indicate a social historicity (de Certeau 1984). Because all meaning is a link in a chain of meaning, and since this chain is infinite, meanings are renewed in interaction—even as they appear to be created for the first time (Bakhtin 1986). Since the conventions and resources of language exceed the immediate context of situated interaction, finding the appropriate context for analyzing the production of meaning becomes conceptually more problematic.

Meaning and knowledge are products of both local application and preexisting interpretive possibilities. Language regards both individual agency and the social organization of knowledge (Smith 1990a, 1999). By examining commonsense knowledge my analyses situate the production of *meaning* in local contexts within the production of *knowledge* in broader cultural contexts. Hence, this book centers questions of knowledge/power by tracing the interconnections between the creative agency of talk and systems of discourse, between the ever-present power of the local context and the generative force of history.

Generally, enthnomethodologists are very critical of impulses to situate ethnomethodological analyses in broader contexts.[21] Despite a great diversity among ethnomethodological studies, there appears to be a broadly shared concern that efforts to expand ethnomethodological analyses, or to use only some aspects of ethnomethodology, can undermine the vision and significance of ethnomethodology (Hilbert 1992, 218–219). These concerns are as long-standing as the scholarly efforts to expand, adapt, or draw from ethnomethodology. For instance, Lemert (1979) argued that ethnomethodology and structuralism (which he designates as including Saussure, Strauss, Foucault, and Derrida) are homologous and should be read intertextually. In addition, Miller (1993, 351) argues that ethnomethodology, in itself, is unable to account for relations of power because such considerations require an analysis that goes beyond the interactional setting to the historical conditions surrounding hegemonic discourses. Similarly, Holstein and Miller

(1993) and Lynch and Bogen (1994) assert that in order to achieve a more comprehensive understanding of social problems, ethnomethodologically-informed analyses need to be linked to broader, interpretative resources. More recently, Moloney and Fenstermaker (2002) explored the relationship between poststructural notions of performativity and ethnomethodological analyses of gender as an interactional accomplishment.

This book joins contemporary research (cf., Holstein and Gubrium 2005; McHoul and Grace 1993) by strategically drawing from ethnomethodology in order to develop an analysis of both local practices and the discursive resources that members bring to bear in local contexts.[22] While the analyses in this book step beyond the notions of evidence required for ethnomethodology, they do not step beyond the interpretative resources shared by cultural members. Because taken-for-granted knowledge saturates both cultures and the individuals that belong to them, it is critically important to push the boundaries of any single research paradigm in order to secure the perspective and vocabulary necessary to understand the production of commonsense.

The analysis of race, class, and gender in this book moves between the production of local meanings on one hand and the production, repetition, and transformation of cultural knowledge on the other. That the analysis is inflected by ethnomethodology and poststructural discourse analysis does not imply that these paradigms can (or should) be fully synthesized. Nor is this analysis intended to diminish the success or importance of either analytical paradigm. All analytical paradigms need to be approached as specialized tools suited for particular purposes.

There is much to be gained by studies that chronicle, within a specific time and place, how meaning is constituted through broad cultural practices that produce both continuity and variation. In effect, to examine how the weight of history bears upon the present moment, both enabling and constraining the possibilities available to us in talk and representation. This study is built upon the principles of inductive analysis. The method is most definitely sociological—even as it tests the boundaries of what counts as sociological.

From Here to There: Theory and Method

The peculiarity of commonsense is that it imposes obviousness—that which we cannot fail to recognize—and, it is this production of obviousness that I examine in a variety of data. To study cultural assumptions requires an innovative research design. Routine knowledge must be produced at every turn in order for it to be unremarkable—

a matter of commonsense. A dependable analysis of commonsense must reveal how interpretative repertoires are deeply rooted to a particular culture and hence requires a highly diverse body of data capable of revealing relationships between local and cultural practices. In order to get at that which most broadly passes as matters of commonsense, my research design includes interviews, newspapers, and television shows.

Within social sciences, the use of multiple data sets can be understood as a form of triangulation intended to increase research validity.[23] The concept of triangulation as a means of validation is rooted to a positivist ontology that understands reality as stable object and that can be accurately observed.[24] However, this study uses two interpretative frameworks that render any simple notion of truth problematic. My aim is not to establish validity for describing "how things objectively are" but to use different data sets to demonstrate how commonsense knowledge comes to make things appear as they do. The use of newspaper, television, and interview data is a "piling" of evidence that produces multiple observations of a single subject (Ragin, Nagel, and White 2003, 16) with the goal of generating the necessary breadth and depth to build empirically-based social theory.

Analytic validation of this research is derived through four considerations: claims that are supported by data and/or logical warrants, detailed analyses not only of patterns but also the exceptions to patterns, coherence with respect to existing debates and fields of knowledge, and a detailed account of findings that enables readers to evaluate each claim (Potter 2004).

My interpretative frameworks of ethnomethodology and poststructural discourse analysis informed the selection of data sets: each of the three data sets that I use to examine meaning-making practices are both discrete and intertwined. In this sense, the variety of data is consistent with the demands of genealogical analysis. Because each medium refracts commonsense knowledge differently (cf., Miller and Fox 2004; Saukko 2003), the combination enriched my ability to locate that, which most broadly passes as assumed knowledge about race, class, and gender in the United States. I treat television, interviews, and newspaper articles as broadly complementary sources of commonsense knowledge about race, class, and gender. By using the same analytical tools to examine media and interviews, I was able to examine the production of taken-for-granted knowledge in local practices and discursive resources in multiple locations. For example, in the process of forging common grounds for communication with others, the media that we actively engage, and the media engaged by others, shapes our conversations and our thinking (Alasutari 1995; Denzin 2002). Consider how phrases like "where's the beef" or "show me the money" creep into the vocabularies of people who have never seen the commercial or film that produced the expressions.

By examining commonsense knowledge, I make a two-fold argument: first inequalities are naturalized and made meaningful through the *routine* production of race, gender, and class in daily life; and second, that language must be analyzed in both local and broader, cultural contexts in order to more fully account for the production of knowledge, power, and culture.

Interviews

I conducted purposive sampling of Web-based organizations, places of employment, homeless shelters, and, occasionally, used personal referrals to create a highly diverse group of interviewees from urban and rural areas of Northern California. In selecting people to be interviewed, I focused on historically constituted categories of difference and included a cross-section of racial categories. Also included among those I interviewed are Jews and ethnic whites, lesbians, bisexuals, people who immigrated as children to the United States, and others who were among first-generation in their families to be born in the United States. I sought a balance of men and women and, in the interests of gender diversity, included transgendered persons.[25] In addition, I sought interviewees from a broad economic range including those who owned nothing more than what they carried with them to those with $500 million in assets. Ages ranged from 23 to 71; some people were parents, and some were grandparents. In all, I conducted 23 in-depth interviews that generated 1,600 pages of transcript. While it was impossible to avoid some categorical overlap among my interviewees (for instance there are five white men), no two interviewees share categorical similarities across axes of race, class, and gender. (See Appendix A for demographics.) The goal of this sampling strategy was to maximize the possibility of locating commonsense knowledge that links people together across commonly understood categories of difference.

At the end of each interview, I invited the interviewee to select a pseudonym that was consistent with his or her gender and racial identity. While some people in the study elected not to use pseudonyms, most chose names they could easily remember, others—such as Captain Ahab and Cuauhtemoc—chose names with special symbolic significance. I attribute all quotes to these pseudonyms.

Newspapers

Initially, I examined 413 randomly selected news stories about homelessness appearing between 1982 and 1996 in three daily metropolitan papers, the *New York Times,* the *Los Angeles Times,* and the *Washington Post.* I selected articles about homelessness for two reasons. First, homelessness is a relatively new discursive formation; these articles provided an opportunity to trace the production of a new social subject. Second, perceptions of wealth and class in passing encounters are largely unreliable, except in the case of absolute poverty. For instance, we may stand beside a multimillionaire in a line at a fast food restaurant without realizing it. Articles about homelessness (like homelessness itself) render class as visible as race and gender. Finally, newspaper articles reveal myriad ways in which reports about "the homeless" rely upon and reproduce commonsense understandings of class. (See Appendix B for more details on data collection of newspaper articles.)

Television Shows

I deliberately selected a variety of televisions shows—as I did interviewees. I began my television data collection in the 1999 fall season with intensive viewing of primetime shows on ABC, NBC, and CBS—because most adult TV viewing occurs during the evening and the major networks are most widely available. Given my analytical interest in commonsense knowledge, my methodological strategies were guided by shows that were most easily attainable; many people do not have access to cable and HBO. If it seems that "everybody" has cable, consider that cable networks develop programming for relatively smaller and more specific audiences. The examples of ESPN, Nickelodeon, and Lifetime come immediately to mind. Evidence of cable's smaller audience size can be found in ratings; advertiser ratings for commercial network programs tend to be nearly three or four times larger than for cable (Museum of Broadcast Communications 2006).

In order to minimize the importance of genre-specific conventions my analysis runs across programming differences in style, content, and market audience. I selected three genres to study: news magazines, situation comedies, and dramas; I then selected three shows from each genre. From seven possible news magazines, I selected *60 Minutes, 60 Minutes II,* and *20/20,* because they make some effort to appear to present "objective news"—focusing on consumer exposés, in-depth coverage of current news stories, and human-interest/personality pieces. From an array of thirty-five half-hour sitcoms, I chose three shows that made some aspect of "difference" apparent within an otherwise homogeneous setting: *The Hughleys, Frasier,* and *Ladies' Man.* From the seven legal dramas featured on network primetime, I selected three one-hour shows that included white women and people of color in central parts: *Judging Amy, Family Law,* and *The Practice.*

Unlike film, television shows repeat over and again through various forms of syndication—even news magazines commonly repeat segments by reshuffling previously run segments into new programs. Consider that the 1999 opening season for *Judging Amy,* which I analyze in this book, was being re-run on TNT in 2005. It is simultaneously available on DVD and can be downloaded, an episode at a time, online. Further, TV series are now being converted to files that can be downloaded on iPods. The extension and intensification of teletechnology has moved television well beyond a broadcast model (Clough 2000, 96). Television has come to inhabit our daily lives, through a variety of technologies. Analyzing television as a singular text misses that television universalizes the circulation of discourses. Television provides, and draws upon, cultural resources for more than immediate audiences. Television collapses distinctions between production and reproduction, between production and circulation, and between text and context (Clough 2000). In a sense, the repetition of TV shows in various formats can be understood to reiterate the repetitions within the shows themselves.[26] Television is less a singular text and more a technological movement and mediation of culture.

Overview of the Book

In the post-civil rights era, effective movements for social justice require an understanding of the performativity of language in relation to the material conditions lived experience. The central theoretical concerns of this book can be summarized by three broad arguments. First, the relative importance of race, gender, and class as social categories—as systems of classification—depends upon, not only their use in a particular context, but their repetition over time in *multiple* local contexts. The productive force of language is anchored through a multiplicity of sites and a repetition of strategies precisely because the relationship between human agency and discursive power is profoundly unstable and in need of constant marking and reinforcement.

Second, commonsense knowledge offers a unique and important analytical framework for understanding race, gender, and class. By examining that which is most broadly assumed about the presence of meaningful difference, it becomes possible to understand the practices and processes through which hegemonic power is naturalized. In addition, because commonsense knowledge necessarily situates individual practices within a cultural context, analyses of commonsense provide an important bridge between studies of local and cultural contexts.

Third, I argue that the schism between studies of talk and theories of language prevents a full analysis of knowledge, power, and agency. Since the possibility of agency and the potential for change exists only in the "everydayness" of living, studies of agency must be grounded in local, material contexts. However, knowledge/power always exceeds the immediate moment and need to be understood through the ability to travel across time and space.

Chapter 2 analyzes how the *presence* of race, rooted to commonsense knowledge, exists as a routine part of our social landscapes, while the *meanings* of race remain conflicted and seemingly unrestrained by the demands of logic, proof, or coherence. I illustrate how the apparently contradictory meanings of race work through commonsense knowledge to stabilize the presence of race and racialized inequalities. Further, I demonstrate how commonsense secures the social, historical, political and economic spaces that give "race" its materiality. Finally, I theorize a two-fold strategy for resisting racism and racialized inequalities.

Chapter 3 explores the coercive force behind the apparent naturalness of gender. I examine how race, gender, class, citizenship, and sexuality are linked discursively and argue that the power of gender comes through constitutive practices that not only produce people as "naturally" women and men, but which also produce heterosexuality, homophobia, xenophobia, racism, and class discrimination. In addition, I demonstrate how, and to what effect, commonsense forces specific erasures of gender. For instance, in interviews and in television shows, discursive practices produced contradictions between being black and being a woman. And, in interviews and newspaper articles, discursive practices rendered people who cannot afford housing as genderless (e.g., the homeless). I broadly situate the analyses of this chapter within the epistemological debates associated with material and poststructural feminisms to argue that an analysis of commonsense knowledge makes it possible to demonstrate how lived experience, and the discourses through which experience is constituted, are analytically and politically linked.

Chapter 4 examines how people and media engage in practices that actively and systematically disorganize the presence of social and economic capital. The overarching analysis of this chapter demonstrates ways in which the material, economic circumstances and the social meanings of class are not ontologically distinct. I elaborate upon the performative aspects of class discourse and explore the relatively new discursive production of "the homeless." I argue that discursive analyses of class positions are a means for understanding how material conditions gain meanings that lead to particular kinds of repetitions and interventions. This chapter closes by proposing a strategy of social change produced through disindentification and which resituates the politics that personalize poverty into the historical conditions that make such poverty both possible and apparently natural.

Chapter 5 provides theoretical and analytical point of departure. After a short overview of the methodological, theoretical, and substantive contributions of this book, I situate my analyses in relationship to their significance for social justice as well as for social sciences in general and sociology in particular. I argue for more and different forms of sociological studies of language. All meaning is produced through language and so it is through studies of language that we can see the processes that constitute the presence, meaning, and value of social life. In short, I argue that scholars can advance an agenda of social justice by working at the constitutive frontiers of language to imagine new socialities and new subjectivities.

2

ROUTINE MATTERS

RACIALIZATION IN EVERYDAY LIFE

Among the social paradoxes of the twenty-first century, is race. In the United States, race is both central and submerged, both "unimportant" and "all consuming," a social fabrication and a material reality. While the presence of race exists as a familiar part of our social landscapes, the *meanings* of race remain conflicted and seemingly unrestrained by the demands of logic, proof, or coherence. In this chapter, I begin with the premise that racialized inequalities come to rest in those things *assumed* to be so real that they are undeserving of thought. For if our ideas about race can be transformed through logic, experience, and argument, commonsense is far more trenchant. For instance, just as we *see* the movement of the sun across the sky, even though we know the sun does not move, commonsense tells us that we still *see* racial differences—in hair, skin, and facial features.

Scholars and activists have been writing about race for more than two hundred years. In the research of W.E.B. Du Bois, Frederick Douglas, and Ida B. Wells, one can see analytical strategies that form the foundations of contemporary social constructionist analysis. However, racism, sexism, and the politics of "scientific knowledge" converged to marginalize much of this research and established positivism and essentialism as the foundations of formal research on race.[1] However, by the late 1960s, particularly in sociology, three successive analytical shifts challenged the existing essentialist framework and produced paradigmatic changes to the positivist epistemological foundations of studies

23

of race: social constructionism (Berger and Luckman 1966), racial formation (Omi and Winant 1994; Roediger 1991, 1994; Saxton 1971, 1990; Wellman 1993), and critical race theory (Crenshaw 1991, 1992; Lopez 1996; Matsuda 1993).[2] Further, ethnomethodology (West 1995a, b, 1999) used an empirical foundation to argue that race is an inter-actional accomplishment. In addition, the cultural turn inaugurated a radical, epistemoligical shift by examining the discursive construction of race (Appiah 1985; Dei, Karumanchery and Karumanchery-Luik 2004; Derrida 1982; Johnson 2003; Pratt 1985). This chapter both builds upon and challenges existing research by analyzing the knowledge that must be assumed for race to be produced recognizably, reliably, and meaningfully across a variety of contexts. While the production of race is always contextually dependent and therefore specific, commonsense knowledge about race, on which local productions rely, must remain more constant in order for the *presence* of race to remain broadly intel-ligible. I argue that if individuals consciously wrestle with the *meanings* of race, at the level of commonsense, historical relations of power inhere in our abilities to recognize race. This chapter deconstructs the logic by which commonsense maintains its authority to secure the recognition of race and concludes with considerations for social change.

Believing is Seeing: Recognizing Race

In this section, I address two questions: How is race produced as a rou-tine matter that requires no elaboration? And, what are the effects of these productions? In short, I analyze both how commonsense consti-tutes people as accountable members of racialized groups and to what effect.[3] Commonsense leads us to believe that we simply see what is there to be seen—to believe that we are observers of an objective social world. For example, in the nine television shows I studied, the appear-ance of race was self-evident to the extent that not one character or person ever demonstrated confusion or difficulty regarding racial cat-egorizations. No one ever asked about another's race nor did anyone incorrectly identify another's race. In this regard, the TV shows that I studied rendered the ability to *recognize* race not only unproblematic but a routine competence expected of all people. Indeed, commonsense knowledge that race can be seen, just by looking at a person, made face-to-face questions about racial identity in my interviews completely absurd for people who identified themselves as white or as black. For instance, when I asked Lana Jacobs about her racial identity, she looked at me in disbelief and *shouted*, "I'm BLACK." To her mind, her racial identity *should have been* obvious to me. Couldn't I *see* that she was black? Lana later remarked—off tape—that she has checked plenty of boxes on forms requesting her racial identity but she had never been asked her racial identity by someone *looking* at her. Commonsense leads us to believe that exposure to a shared reality will clarify for all what is true—in this case the "reality" of Lana's "blackness." To Lana it seemed impossible that I could *fail* to see her race as anything except black. Commonsense does not truck in ambiguities or complexities. Polard Parker had a similar reaction when I asked if he had a racial identity.

Polard:	Do I? I don't know. Do I?
Celine-Marie:	I'm asking YOU.
Polard:	Well they ask me to check something on forms every now and then that says white.
Celine-Marie:	So that's what you check?
Polard:	Well I mean, YEAH [makes a face at me as if to indicate that he thinks his response should be obvious].[4]

Polard's response indicates his expectation that his whiteness is obvious. He is able to turn the question of his own identity back at *me,* only if he believes that his race is clearly recognizable. Polard's response also indicates his discomfort with naming himself as white; he consistently resisted calling himself white, choosing instead to insinuate it ("Well they ask me to check something on forms every now and then that says white"). Polard's final and sarcastic response seems to express frustration at what *should have been* obvious to me in the first place.[5]

Unlike interviews, the mention of race in newspaper articles is guided by published industry standards. For instance, the style manuals for the *New York Times*, the *Washington Post*, and United Press International (UPI) each prescribe that race should be cited *only when it is pertinent and its pertinence is clear to the reader* (Siegal and Connolly 1999; UPI 1992; Webb, 1978). Specifically, the *New York Times* style manual, notes:

> ...[the] race of a victim of a hate crime or the subject of a police search is clearly germane, an essential part of the person's description. But the race of a person convicted of a crime is not pertinent unless the case has racial overtones; if it does, the overtones should be explained (Siegal and Connolly 1999, 283).

UPI and the *Washington Post* style manuals advise journalists in very similar ways.[6] However, despite these journalistic guidelines, news articles I examined did include casual references to race. For instance: "a homeless black man" (Terry 1995); "Gary, from a poor black family" (Rimer 1985); and, "one of the homeless—a 35-year-old Chinese refugee" (Ferrell and Nazario 1993). Reporters described people by race without any apparent hesitancy and without elaborating on how they knew the race of the person about whom they wrote. Nor did reporters clarify, or comment on, the *relevance* of the racial categorizations they reported. However, not all races were casually noted. While reporters might refer to "a homeless black man" (Terry 1995), as noted earlier, in fifteen years of articles about homelessness, I found no comparable references to "a homeless white man." Whiteness was the assumed, or unmarked, category.

The practice of casually noting some races, but not all, constitutes those *particular* racial characterizations as inherently meaningful. And, because reporters do not explain why they make particular racial categorizations in a given story, they require readers to provide the relevant racial meanings. The *meanings* of race are left apparently blank for readers to fill-in. It is possible to mark race without explanation precisely because the meaning of race always exceeds the context in which it is invoked. The effect of routine racial categorizations in newspapers is to naturalize race as *inherently* relevant. To the extent that whiteness is an unmarked racial category, it appears to be irrelevant. Whiteness thus is produced as a "normal" way of being.

The only occasions in which news articles characterized persons as white were those involving racialized conflict. Consider, for instance, "On the first day of school one of the black children from a homeless family struck a white township youngster" (Sullivan 1988). In this example, the writer characterizes "one of the black children" as belonging to a "homeless family" (i.e., questionably part of the community) but writes about "a white *township* youngster"(i.e., someone who clearly belongs to the community). With these characterizations, it would be difficult to mistake the newsworthy nature of this story as being a schoolyard fight among children. While writing about children, the reporter tells a story about belonging that centers the conflict on issues of race, poverty, and community. Since newspaper articles about homelessness only characterized people as white in relationship to racialized conflict, whiteness functioned as much a marker of racialized *conflict* as it did a category of race. Whiteness emerged as a subject position produced through, or made visible by, racialized conflict.

In fifteen years of newspaper articles about homelessness, I did not find any references to Latinos, Mexicans, or Hispanics who were homeless—even though people without housing often had Spanish surnames such as Cisneros (Pinsky 1985), Rivera (Nix 1986), Martinez, and Gonzalez (Purdy 1994). One might argue that Spanish surnames can, in themselves, mark race/ethnicity—as a matter of commonsense—particularly in urban metropolitan areas. However, this was true *only* for Spanish surnames. For instance, Mr. Huang was characterized as "a Chinese refugee" (Ferrell and Nazario 1993). While this practice may reflect expectations that most readers in the United States are not able to distinguish among Asian names, it also assumes that such recognition or distinction has inherent importance to stories of homelessness.

Reporting practices rely upon, and reproduce, commonsense knowledge that race is both self-evident and meaningful. Consequently, reporting practices ensure that race remains a central component of cultural discourse, while allowing readers to assess exactly *why* race is meaningful.[7] This is especially significant because race is a "floating signifier" or a "loose term" that depends upon a particular relationship for meaning. Loose terms can only be understood in relation to something else. Broadly speaking, because all words and concepts depend on relationships and contexts for meaning, all meaning floats—all language is loose. However, some words are more easily fixed than others. While the meaning of loose terms, or floating signifiers, can be temporarily fixed, no single definition will function in all contexts. The looseness of race makes articles that invoke race, reflexive—in this sense, the subject and object become fused through the interpretative processes that make the mention of race meaningful.

While commonsense leads us to believe that accounts describe an objective social world, it is *through* our accounts that we produce a sense of what is true, relevant, and meaningful. Accounts do not describe things with more or less accuracy; rather, accounts "establish what is accountable in the setting in which they occur" (Handel 1982, 36). Mentions of race in newspaper articles about homelessness, then, should be understood—not as *describing* people by race but—as making people potentially *accountable* by race. Because whiteness was not marked in newspaper articles about homelessness, white people were not made potentially accountable by race as routinely as were people of color. In this sense, commonsense knowledge constitutes race as both presence and erasure; this is why erasures must be understood, and treated, as another kind of production central to the meanings of race.

That race appeared to be self-evident in interviews and media speaks to how the history and the politics of race remain deeply submerged in daily life. The apparently self-evident nature of race is evidence that race *has relevant* meaning, rather than that it has any *particular* meaning. This cleavage between relevance and meaning is possible because the presence of race is itself an effect of power. A system of oppression racialized particular phenotypes. In this sense, the categories of race, in and of themselves, can be understood as expressions of racism (cf., Memmi 2000).

If racism is the *source* of race, one can argue endlessly about the *equality* of the races but to no avail. "Racism simply reinvents race and racism through its appropriated power to legitimize, to grant or withhold legitimacy, effectively reproducing the double binds that are the hallmarks of the power to negatively racialize" (Martinot 2003, 26). On one hand, it is essential to understand how the social, economic, and cultural institutions of racism and white supremacy are produced and reproduced through the routine recognition of race. Yet, on the other hand, it is not enough to simply say race is itself an expression of racism. For instance, while race marks relations of privilege, exploitation, and subordination, it *also* provides many people a sense of identity, community, and history (Smith 1998). For many people of color, a refusal of race can express self-loathing—an "assault against ourselves and our community" (Smith 1998, 181–182). However, by identifying with racial categories, even as a way to organize for racial justice, we repeat the problems of racism by reifying race. To the extent that resistance to racism must be articulated through the same discourse it resists (i.e., race), efforts to end racism become complicit with racism itself. Resistance to hegemony is always compromised because the terms of resistance are produced by the terms of domination. If the paradox of race is seemingly irrepressible, I would argue this is true only if we attempt to understand its many manifestations through a single analytical frame.

The central problematic of "difference" encompasses two analytic tensions: one material and one discursive. In a material analytical frame, the lived experience of "difference" is predicated on sameness within social categories (e.g., women, or whites) and differences between categories (women and men, blacks and whites). This conception of difference is not only an expression of commonsense knowledge, it also infuses scholarship in which "difference" is assumed, or argued, to originate from historical, cultural, or biological distinctions that are held to have very wide repercussions in society. The political project of social justice, derived from notions of "difference" based on history, culture, or biology attempts to equalize inequalities between categories—this has been the premise of social justice movements.

In contrast, a poststructural analytical framework refuses to engage at the level of experience—arguing that all experience is already an interpretation of events (Scott 1991). Because all experience is itself discursively structured, poststructuralism's analytical concern is discursive and directed toward rupturing the binaries of "difference." Binary oppositions are constructions which value one side of the binary over the other and create an illusion of complementarity (cf., Butler 1990, 1993, 1995; Derrida 1976; Foucault 1980; Sedgwick 1990; Seidman 1994). Deconstruction demonstrates how power works through language by revealing the illusion of binaries such as white/nonwhite, man/woman where each "half" is taken to be the opposite of the other. Further, poststructural analyses challenge the notion of a modern, unified, human subject upon which "difference" can rest—which leads to the theorization of fluid, fractured, and multiple subject positions and identifications offered by postmodern theories.

The ability to simply recognize race is evidence of how commonsense inscribes on bodies historically forged relations of power, oppression, and exploitation. A crucial function of commonsense knowledge about "difference" is to make discriminatory categories, not just easy to use, but possible to use without thought—because they have become naturalized as self-evident. History is its most seductive and coercive when it reproduces the past without words (Seed 2001). In order to resist the production of commonsense knowledge that renders race self-evident, a refusal to "see" race—as in notions of colorblindness—might seem logical. However colorblindness extends inequities by ignoring or disregarding the importance and impact of historical relations of power (cf., Lopez 1996; Lipsitz 1998; Omi and Winant 1994). Race blindness would in effect extend historical relations of power by reducing systematic inequalities to arbitrary inequalities (Bonilla-Silva 2003; Guinier and Torres 2003). Indeed, "colorblindness" is characteristic of white people's relationship to their own racial identity (Guinier and Torres 2002) and is the very premise of white privilege.

Resistance to racism and racial inequality must begin with practices that remove whiteness from the unmarked center of daily life. This requires a two-fold strategy of disidentification. Pêcheux (1982) drew from Freud, Lacan, and Althuser to elaborate the concept of disidentification.[8] For the purposes of this book, the link to Althuser is most relevant. Althuser argued that subjects are constituted through ideology, in part, by being subjected and tied to an imaginary identity relative to real relations. The relation is imaginary because it works through recognition and identification. Although it is impossible to escape the productive force of hegemonic discourse, disidentification actively works to subvert the prevailing practices of articulation. Disidentification can be understood as a process of rethinking and reconstructing discourses in ways that expose what the hegemonic discourse conceals (Muñoz 1998). In this sense, disindentification, uses hegemonic discourses as raw material for representing a sociality or positionality that had been rendered unthinkable by the dominant culture. It accounts for and includes what dominant discourse marginalizes.

Thinking through the process of disidentification, the most effective strategies intended to resist racism and racialized inequalities will be those which refuse to allow the meaning of race to "float" as everything and nothing. This is not to say that race must come to mean one thing or another but that *the meanings of race must be made visible through the relationships that produce it.* Second, the politics of disidentification require a specific refusal of the apparent naturalness of whiteness by including whiteness—a white racial category, not simply white people—more visibly in public discourse. (The proliferation of white people on television is the product of white hegemony, not disidentification.) In the following section, I examine the production of whiteness and white racial identities.

The Hegemony of Whiteness

Those who have suffered at the boot heel of white racism have long established critiques of whiteness; most recently Hortense Spillers, Cherrie Moraga, Angela Davis, Gloria Anzaldúa, and Akasha Hull have been among scholars and activists of color who have kept white racism and white privilege in the forefront of social critique long before "critical whiteness studies" emerged in the social sciences. The epistemological ground of contemporary critical whiteness studies (cf., Bonilla-Silva 2003; Foley 1997; Frankenberg 1993, 1997a, b; hooks 1992; Ignatiev 1995; Lipsitz 1998; Perry 2004; Roediger 2002; Ware 1992; Wellman 1993) is a social constructionist framework that flexibly engages both racial formation theory and critical race theory. While the work of critical white studies is to disrupt the unmarked status of whiteness, the results have been uneven, at times serving to recenter and reprivilege the lives and perspectives of white people. However, by and large, critical whiteness studies have made important contributions to critiques of whiteness. Across disciplines, abundant literature provides rich analyses of the social, historical, legal, and economic processes through which a white racial identity has been constructed and important critiques of the inseparability of whiteness from strategies of racial dominance. More recently, scholars have begun to deconstruct whiteness as a practice rather than a characteristic (cf., Aanerud 2003; Chabram-Dernersesian 2003; Muraleedharan 2003) giving rise to the distinction between being white and whiteness as something that is achieved.

This section examines the practices through which whiteness is produced as a routine matter of daily life. For instance, across fifteen years of newspaper articles, twenty-three interviews, and eight (of nine) television shows, whiteness was *never* noted as a routine racial category. Existing literature provides an understanding of how the unmarked nature of whiteness produces and maintains white racial dominance, yet we have little understanding of the more nuanced practices through which whiteness is produced as unmarked. Exactly how does whiteness gain meaning, not as a racial category, per se, but rather as a kind of "normalcy," an invisible center from which "difference" can be measured? How does commonsense knowledge lead to practices that make whiteness both invisible *and* culturally meaningful? What gives whiteness, as a generally unmarked category, interpretative stability? I take up these and other questions by examining commonsense knowledge about white racial identities.

Who Me? White People and Racial Identity

Although all of my interviewees talked about race as self-evident, people who identified themselves as white on my interview exit form all appeared to be uncomfortable when talking about race during the interview. For example, in response to my question about the meaning of race, Ashley Worthington explained:

> Umm I have um [long pause] well I don't know. And I think that's a particularly white way of asking what, er—responding to that cuz I don't really know what, I mean I think maybe I do because it's, it's, it's dealing a lot with a ...with a...[short pause] with a cultural difference that I that I only have a very, very limited knowledge of, I think, I mean, I think as much as I TRY to be sensitive to things and uh and uh traditions and all these other things, I think I have a very limited knowledge of it. And um, even with my, my consciousness—er...er, my consciousness raised, I just I still think I have a very, very limited knowledge of what race is.

The pauses, stammers, and sputters that are typically removed from interview transcripts to make them easier to read are central to conveying Ashley's palpable discomfort. She begins by linking her ignorance about race to whiteness ("I think that's a particularly white way of asking what, er—responding") and seems to imply that only white people would *not* know about race. When Ashley says "I TRY to be sensitive to things" and refers to being a person who has had her "consciousness raised," she makes herself recognizable as someone who, although if somewhat ignorant, has made an effort (arguably, a well-intentioned effort) to learn about race. Underlying Ashley's talk about having a very limited knowledge of race, despite her best efforts, is an understanding of race as something that unknown *others* possess. Whiteness emerges in her talk as an un-raced position from which things about race can be learned. And in this sense, she links together her ignorance about race, her good intentions to learn about race, and a kind of innocence—she appears not to be implicated in matters of race.

I asked everyone I interviewed if she or he had a racial identity. Only white people responded with questions such as: "Who, me?" or "Me, personally?" Given that there were only two people present in each interview, each of us recognizably white, I had to consider these questions more rhetorical than substantive. They do not refer to a confusion regarding about whom I was asking, but rather to the fact that I was asking at all. While this might be understood as an expression of the self-evident nature of race, it was also congruent with general levels of disinterest and confusion that white people demonstrated regarding their racial identities. Whiteness—for white people—appeared to have no meaning as a race category. For instance only people, who identified themselves as white, talked about their race category as a matter of forms and boxes. Consider this exemplar from Lue Lani:

> Every form you fill out now is asking you this question all the time. And when it asks you, it tells you—are you white, are you Mexican, are you this, are you that? And you have to go down and it's sort of like, I think we're imprinting it upon ourselves that there IS, gee I'm over here in this one.

By talking about racial identity as something produced by a form, Lue Lani both constructs, and relies upon, a sense of race as unimportant or irrelevant to her daily life. If her characterization that we are "imprinting" race upon ourselves resists the reification of race, her characterization "gee I'm over here in this one" also serves to minimize the importance of racialized identities. In this excerpt race is stripped both of historical significance and of current political, social, and economic importance.

Since it might seem that only a white person could claim to take her racial identity from a form, it is also important to remind oneself of the importance of U.S. census categories in creating racialized identities. Racial categories such as quadroons and octoroons no longer circulate in public discourse, although they once were reified as social identities, in part, through the U.S. census. Indeed this complex history has been at the center of contemporary debates regarding the politics of the U.S. census.

When Betty Sakurai, who identified herself as Japanese-American, talked about her racial identity, whiteness again posed a blank space. Betty characterized her mother as white and her father as Japanese. She talked at length about family rituals and customs that she enjoys that come from the Japanese side of her family but said "from my mom's side there wasn't, we didn't have a lot of cultural things at all."[9] She concluded her reflection this way:

> I don't know, its just I—I LOVE the fact that I am half ANYTHING, you know. I think whatever it was, I would totally embrace it and want to learn more and more about it and I—I just I love it.

Although Betty identifies herself as biracial, she talked about "Japanese" as a racial category but not "white" ("I LOVE the fact that I am half ANYTHING"). Whiteness—her mother's side of the family—is the blank space that allows Betty to be "half anything." Whiteness emerges as the space against which racial categories gain meaning and visibility. In hegemonic U.S. culture, whiteness comes to stand as the "ordinary" way of being human (cf., Frankenberg 1997b). Since discourse constitutes subjugated subjectivities by marking "difference" from an unspoken hegemonic center, the visible processes that mark or name what they point to always constitute subjects as "others." This excerpt demonstrates one way that local practice can produce the invisibility of whiteness while maintaining whiteness as a hegemonic "center"—from which all distances are measured by marked categories. Betty's celebration of being "half anything" also extends the disciplinary power of whiteness.

In U.S. television programs, as in interviews, representational practices also produced whiteness as the daily context on which racial issues may be overlaid. For example, in *Judging Amy,* Bruce Van Axel works as a court services officer for Judge Amy Gray. He is an apparently black man whose most significant speaking parts, in the 1999 season, were attempts to educate Amy, an apparently white woman, about race. In these conversations, Amy takes shelter in idealism while Bruce informs her with restrained anger about reality.

Amy: Maybe I am idealistic enough to hope that we will have a society where race isn't the bottom line.

Bruce: Until you have a child come home and tell you she was called a nigger you can't understand how impossible that is (aired November 12, 1999).

Significantly, Bruce animates the racial slur; as the only black cast member in this season he is the only person in the show who cannot be made responsible for the reiterative wounds of white racism. For Judge Amy Gray, as for the white people I interviewed, *ignorance* about race is made to stand as a claim to a kind of innocence, which in this case, is related to idealism. Amy doesn't have to see, and appears to be not implicated, in the disparity between what she and what Bruce each experience as ordinary. In addition, this excerpt illustrates how people who are not recognizably white are made responsible for, and carriers of, that which is not ordinary or innocent—that which is raced. The disciplinary power of whiteness in television was exercised both through its invisibility and through its ability to impose a kind of compulsory visibility on those who are not white.

In U.S. television shows, the concerns, interests, and needs of white people appeared as a kind of "normalcy" against which racialized lives became "different." In TV drama (*Family Law, Judging Amy,* and *The Practice*) and situation comedies (*Ladies Man* and *Frasier*), whiteness functioned as an unmarked condition of normalcy. Whiteness was produced as a "normal" or ordinary way of being, both through the overwhelming presence of white people and through the way that whiteness consistently passed without remark. The apparent normalcy of whiteness on network TV also was produced by casting apparently white actors as characters with speaking roles and casting actors who appear to be "of color" in nonspeaking roles that were incidental to scenes—much like props that comprise a background for the story lines. Consider that in *Frasier*, two black characters appeared in the 1999 season: a TV news anchorwoman, who appeared on Frasier's TV set, and a woman waiting tables in the café he frequented. Only *The Hughley's*—a comedy about a black family in a predominantly white neighborhood—produced whiteness as a marked category.

However, analyzing whiteness creates a methodological problem: how to analyze the productive force of erasure? The commonsense erasure of whiteness left little or no evidence in the local context, no quotes of people calling themselves or others white, no interactions in which whiteness appeared to be relevant. The local context, by itself, could not provide empirical access to the power of whiteness because whiteness functioned as both a routine and privileged subject position. For instance, whiteness was produced through the saturation of opportunities, the success of hard work, the adequacy of good intentions, the comfort of having police, and the confidence that one's best effort will be good enough. For example, in *Judging Amy*, the character of Vincent Gray is a struggling writer who wins the Pushcart Prize for fiction and obtains a book contract from a large publisher. Although he suffers great existential angst, he meets with significant professional success at every turn. Whiteness was a saturation of privilege that formed the background—not the focus—of TV shows. Apparently white people were never represented in ways that associated them with chronic poverty, discrimination, or daily drudgery. The only apparently white people who appeared to experience any degree of economic hardship were senior citizens seeking cheaper prescription medications in Canada in a *60 Minutes* (aired October 17, 1999) news segment.[10]

The power of whiteness—for white people—works through virtue of its invisibility, through the ability of commonsense to erase the presence and meaning of white racial identities and to produce all other racial identities as apparently inherently meaningful—even if the meanings of those racialized identities are unclear or contradictory. In a white cultural imagination, commonsense knowledge (re)produces biological essentialism by masking or silencing the articulation of social, historical, and economic processes that make whiteness meaningful. Whiteness gains interpretive stability because its meanings are anchored to a former biological notion of race that produces the commonsense understanding that whiteness is what one *sees*.

By reifying "difference," while simultaneously denying its importance, discursive practices promote a kind of pluralism that leaves race and racism intact. Indeed, the racism of white liberalism functions through practices that withhold ordinariness from people who are "not white" (Memmi 2000). This denial of ordinariness is a cornerstone of liberal racism—I say *liberal* racism because it operates at a level of assumption, rather than at the level of belief or intention. By denying ordinariness to people of color, hegemonic commonsense knowledge produces a racialized vernacular moral order.

Yes, You: A Counter-Hegemonic Production of Whiteness

Without question, my own presence as a white person shaped my data collection and analysis in ways that, at times, must have exceeded my awareness. That none of my interviewees engaged in what could be called counter-hegemonic productions of whiteness might be a result of my own presence as a visibly white person. As one might expect, across fifteen years of newspaper articles about homelessness, none included counter-hegemonic productions of whiteness. And, of the nine TV shows I studied, only *The Hughley's* treated whiteness as a marked category.

Recall that in newspaper articles, whiteness became a marked category only in reports of racial conflict; in *The Hughley's*, whiteness was marked with reference to historicized, racialized conflict. For instance, Darryl and his brother Milsap invite Dave (Darryl's white neighbor) to go out with them on Halloween (aired October 26, 1999). Dave thanks Darryl and Milsap for the invitation, and Darryl responds: "I had to invite you cause two black guys sneaking around the neighborhood ain't gonna fly unless there's a white guy to vouch for them." Here, as whiteness loses its unmarked status—its naturalness— it also loses its innocence. In black imagination, whiteness is often a representation—not of innocence—but of terror (hooks 1992). The historical cultural meanings that produced whiteness must, to some extent, be part of the enunciation that makes whiteness visible, if such enunciations are to avoid re-inscribing white supremacy. To make whiteness visible is to reveal its coercive force (cf., Roediger 1994).

Consider another episode in which Darryl's grandmother, Hattie Mae, invited Dave and his family to join her extended family for Thanksgiving dinner (aired November 5, 1999). When Dave and his family arrive, they are the only white characters on the set and their little boy announces: "Dad says we're gonna be the only white folks for miles and miles." The camera settles on the Hughley family standing motionless as they stare in shock and anger until Dave delivers the punch line: "I did NOT however say that was a bad thing." A sound track of laughter accompanies the resuming action. The humor in this scene draws from the child's ability to speak the truth that lays bare the framework of racism, which exceeds his understanding. Consider also how commonsense knowledge provides the central context for the humor of this scene. For instance, the audience needs no explanation of why Dave noted that they were "gonna be the only white folks for miles and miles." Indeed the Hughley family response demonstrates their emotionally concordant reading this comment. The punch line delivers a laugh because it articulates what the audience believes to be literally true ("I did NOT however say that was a bad thing"), while concealing an historically-rooted emotional truth: a white fear of black people. Dave did not *need* to say it would be a "bad thing." The scene raises the ghost of racism and renders it impotent but not meaningless. The meanings of whiteness in *The Hughley's* are produced *in relationship* to the meanings of blackness—both through a shared history that permeates their relationships and through characters' abilities to parlay that history into a different present. In this sense, *The Hughley's* resists dominant discursive practices that constitute white people as both innocent and without race. *The Hughley's* did not represent people of color as being accountable for "explaining" race and racism to whites, nor did it reproduce a racial binary that implicates people of color as "the opposite" of white people—i.e., that which is not innocent or ordinary. By making the *meanings* of whiteness as visible as the *presence* of whiteness, *The Hughley's* produced a counter-hegemonic discourse through which a cultural transformation of race could become possible.

The Uncommon Presence of Race

While the marking of race in interviews and in media was a routine matter that required no elaboration or comment with respect to categories such as black, African American, Latino, or Asian, this was not the case with respect to Native Americans. Across newspapers and interviews, Native American people were never categorized by race as a matter of routine "observation." In this section, I examine how talk and representation, in interviews and news articles, produced the presence and meaning of Native American racial identities. I do not include television analysis because in the fall season of 1999 none of the nine, network television shows that I studied included Native American people or issues. Yet the erasure of Native American people and issues on television does not stand entirely apart from the patterns that appeared in newspaper articles. Reporting practices in news articles about homelessness employed discursive practices that constituted American Indian identity as a part of the historical past rather than as a part of the national present.

Although reporters' racial characterizations of people as "black" or "Chinese" are embedded in news stories as unremarkable observations that apparently anyone would understand, their characterizations of a person as "Native American" were elaborated upon. For example, the description of a person as Native American seemed to affect nearly every detail of how the story of homelessness was told. One article described a small group of "reservation-born" Native Americans living under an overpass as: a "little band of urban nomads" living in makeshift shelters that were "lovingly constructed" and of which "a more accurate description might be wooden hogans" (Cohen 1984, 1). The reference to "reservation-born" lets readers know these are "real" Native Americans and marks authenticity as central to Native American identity. In addition, because dominant white discourse about Native Americans creates a romantic oneness with nature—the reporter writes as if Native American heritage explains the superior construction of their shelter ("hogans") and a sense of community ("band of urban nomads")—in short, their success in adapting to living without housing.

Although reporting practices rely on commonsense to make racial categorizations meaningful, in articles that reference Native American people there is a presumed lack of familiarity, which translates into a racialized exoticism. In addition, this racialized exoticism is imbricated with an essentialist discourse of authenticity—recall the reference to people as "reservation-born." To more fully understand the work accomplished through discourses of racial authenticity, I turn to my interviews with people who identified themselves as Native Americans, all of whom raised issues of authenticity regarding themselves as well as others who self-identified as Native Americans.

Lorraine Doe, a member of the Paiute Nation, recalled an incident in which young Native Americans were "irate" over a flyer full of racial stereotypes that advertised "an Indian medicine woman" coming to their area. In the following excerpt, Lorraine is recalling part of her conversation when she met with a group of young Native Americans who wanted to organize a protest:

> [I said] "First, let's make sure that the person really IS a Native American medicine woman." So, I called the number, found out who it was, I called that person, talked to her, and just said, "You know, we're checking up on this, given that this is California, and there's all these plastic crystal Indians out here. You know, we wanna just make sure that honor is given to the— you know, to this population a— as a Native American person, you're probably EQUALLY as concerned. Um, so, help us out here. And, gimme a call back, and let's talk." ... And so, the lady called me back, and she said, "Yes, as a Native American person, I'm very, very concerned about, you know, authenticity. And by the way, I'm not Native American, I'm a RAINBOW PERSON."

Through a strategic sequence, Lorraine first claims her authority as a Native American person to investigate the authenticity of those who advertise themselves as such. She frames her concerns in terms of honor, and makes her intolerance for non-Native peoples appropriating Native American spirituality clear, by referring to "plastic crystal Indians," and yet without directly impugning the person she is calling. Lorraine invokes her authority as a Native American a second time by framing her concern as one that *any* other Native American would share and skillfully corners the self-proclaimed medicine woman. Through this sequence, Lorraine challenges a deceitful practice and establishes a way for the woman to save face as an ally with shared concerns, which the woman accepts and then acknowledges her deceit. This story does more than stop one more "plastic crystal Indian." Part of the interactional work that marginalized people often learn as a survival skill is the manipulation of conversational ambiguities (cf., Miller 1993). In recounting this story to younger Native Americans who had wanted to mount a protest, Lorraine demonstrates a careful strategy of resistance honed, by centuries of genocide and appropriation, into a deft confrontation without aggression.

Daily strategies of resistance to domination permeated all of my interviews with Native Americans. And all Native American people I interviewed, invoked discourses of authenticity in some way to resist domination and exploitation. Consider this excerpt from my interview with Rudy Rosales, who identified himself as American Indian. Rudy had come to the interview with what he called his "pedigree"—a genealogy that traced his family lineage back hundreds of years. He put it this way

> I wish people would say, [claps] 'Ok you're Native American Indian [...] do you have any kind of proof of that Indian part?' And that way we'd get rid of a lot of riff raff. [...] And that way the people that don't have proof would sit there with their tongues hangin' out of their mouth and I would sit there goin' here's my proof. You know, I've done my homework. You know, now you guys don't have it? I'm not gonna hold it against them—but you know at least I've proven who I am, you know. And if you guys have to—or not HAVE to—but you guys SHOULD acknowledge ME before you acknowledge any of these people because I have, and they're as—the way I felt—if they're as proud of their heritage as I am, they'd do this.

Implicit in Rudy's discussion is concern with the proliferation of non-Native people who appropriate Native American cultural heritage. Identity for Rudy is a kind of boundary that requires policing in the form of "proof." As Rudy insists that he will not "hold it against" people who have no proof, he appeals to the authority of non-Native people to do exactly that—indeed white people in the United States have been in the very business of "authenticating" Native American identities through blood quanta for nearly two centuries. In particular, I understand the tensions Rudy articulates through notions of "proof" and "pedigree" as part of a larger context in which competition for authenticity is fostered by the U.S. government's policy toward Native American entitlements. In a world in which race is apparently self-evident, Rudy has been working for years to gain recognition from the federal government for his tribal nation—for their racial identity.

Although blood once held mythic abilities (e.g., nobility, courage, and virtue), racism centers notions of blood on degeneracy (Foucault 1980). Because the notion of blood as race carries *both* of these meanings, Rudy is able to turn the very discourse used *against* Native Americans (and other racialized groups) back upon the society that requires him to produce his "pedigree." Although the discourses of blood quanta and authenticity were generated as a means of domination, interviews with Native American people illustrate how oppressive power can be redeployed—how power circulates as a force that both constrains and constitutes the very possibilities of volition. While the struggle for authenticity emerged in my research with respect to Native American experience, it is a struggle that marginalized people frequently face, although in different ways. For example, while the "one drop rule" has been enough to make one legally black in the United States, "authentic blackness" has always been contested within black communities as well as white (Johnson 2004, 4). The struggle for authenticity is both possible and relentless precisely because there is no "real," no race that resides in bodies. There is a politics to be struggled for in the representation and invocation of authenticity that is both a means to resist, and an extension of, domination itself.

Hegemonic commonsense knowledge about race operates in specific ways with respect to Native Americans. This is evidenced by the complete erasure of Native American people and issues in television, as well as by newspaper reporting practices that racialized Native Americans as exotic "others" whose contemporary presence was both "authenticated" and historicized. These practices ultimately displace Native Americans from public discourse and (re)produce Native Americans as historical, rather than contemporary peoples. Given this cultural context, it's no wonder that the Native Americans I interviewed demonstrated a skilled resistance against continued marginalization.

In the moments in which race is not self-evident, the politics of race begin to surface. Discourse about authenticity regarding Native Americans calls up blood quanta and the legal sanctions against inter-racial marriages intended to preserve some blood lines and the genocidal efforts to destroy others. Beneath self-evident racial categorizations are public stories that describe the world in politically loaded ways (Lubiano 1992). This is precisely why strategies for resisting racism must involve enunciating meanings and relationships—making the meaning of race at any given moment, *more* visible, rather than less—making the meanings of race a matter of discussion, not a matter of commonsense.

Beyond Reason and Coherence: The Meanings of Race

In the first section of this chapter, I demonstrated how commonsense knowledge produces the apparently self-evident nature of race, and examined how the commonsense recognition of race covers over the struggles of race. However, the easy recognition of racialized differences secured by commonsense quickly gave way to apparently irreconcilable and contradictory talk about race. In this section, I focus on the contradictory meanings of race that emerged in interviews to explore how commonsense knowledge is implicated in the competing and contradictory conceptions of race that circulate in public discourse.

The people I interviewed talked about race either as a matter of color, blood, nationality, or culture. Zach Mauro, who identified himself as Filipino, put it this way, "Well when I see race, it's like I see colors. Black...It goes from white to nationalities, Spanish, European categories like that and then this way, African...." Zach places color and nationality on a continuum, as if they are different degrees of the same thing, and presents "African" as a counterpoint to whiteness and white ethnic categories. The way Zach talks about racial categories reflects the visual basis of his racial categorizations. However, beneath the surface of his talk is a commonsense understanding of race that enables him to list "black," "white," "Spanish," "European," and "African" as comparable elements. Notably, Zach indicated "European" as a racial group, not German or French, and "African," not Nigerian or Egyptian. All nationalities do not comprise distinct racial categories. Inherent in his assertion of race as *nationality* is an understanding of which nations (and continents) comprise distinct racial groups.

Consider an excerpt from my interview with Captain Ahab, born in Canada and raised in the United States. His childhood transition between the two countries has held lasting trauma for him, and, at age 53, Captain Ahab still characterized himself "foremost as an immigrant."

> *Captain Ahab:* When I think of race, I generally think of ethnic background.
> *Celine-Marie:* What is that, ethnic background?
> *Captain Ahab:* The culture from which the individual has emerged. The culture in which they grew up which may or may not be defined geographically.
> *Celine-Marie:* Mmmhm. Do you have a racial or ethnic identity?
> *Captain Ahab:* Uh a I regard myself as Caucasian.
> *Celine-Marie:* What does that mean to you?
> *Captain Ahab:* It means coming from essentially white northern European stock.

Given that Captain Ahab talks about racial/ethnic identity as *cultural*, one would expect him to characterize himself by some cultural, or perhaps national, identity (such as Canadian or American). And, given the distinction that he makes between culture and geography, one might also expect him to identify himself as belonging to a broadly dispersed notion of culture, such as a white culture. Yet, despite his characterization of race as ethnicity/culture, he describes himself in biological terms ("as Caucasian"). Captain Ahab's use of "white northern European *stock*" reinforces a sense of racial groups as recognizably distinct "breeds" of people. His talk about race as "culture" is predicated on a discursive framework that establishes race as a biological or genetic difference. Theories of social construction and biological essentialism do not exist in opposition to each other. Rather, biological essentialism *is rearticulated* through social constructionist analyses that are rooted to culture and history. Even as talk about race shifts from biology to culture, the same false sense of homogeneity follows race (Appiah and Gutman 1996).

In the United States, discourses of race intertwine with, and are sometimes produced through, discourses of immigration and national origin. In my interviews, nationality was talked about as a racial category for countries that had been exploited by colonial relationships—e.g., Spaniards are white but Mexicans are not. Colonial expansion advanced notions of race, nation, and culture by linking imperial power to images of savages—both to promote power and notions of homeland purity (Gilroy 2000). In this sense, race can be understood as a visual symbol of empire. By creating the *impression* of social unities that are both homogeneous and anonymous, racial categories articulate historical relations of domination and oppression (Guillaumin 1995).

Since racial categorizations are fundamentally about historical, political, and cultural alliances, exploitations, and identifications, it is possible for both "European" and "Mexican" to *function* as racial categories. However, because national heritage is not readily observable, the notion of race as national heritage seems to contradict the self-evident (i.e., visual) nature of race produced by commonsense. Yet both are premised on the same discursive formation; the essentialist notion of race, once attributed to biology, continues to naturalize ideologies of "difference" when it emerges through an essentialist notion of nationhood (Appiah 1992, 5). This connection between biology and nationhood is the unarticulated link in Zach's talk that produces a racial continuum that can move from "colors to nationalities."

While interviewees easily talked about race as skin color, this conception of race relied on taken-for-granted knowledge that also appeared to be full of contradictions. Not all differences—or similarities—in skin color were tied to racial categories. For example, although Italians are no longer commonly considered a distinct racial group, Emerson Piscopo, an Italian-American, mentioned several times that he did not consider Italians to be white.

Celine-Marie: Tell me about Italians not being white.

Emerson: Um, well, most of us have that olive dark skin [half laugh] dark skin.

Celine-Marie: Uh-huh.

Emerson: You know, I see white as being a really, as, as being, being really white. You know, like somebody who's not um of your, from European—like dark skin, I'm talking about dark skin, dark eyes, dark hair.[…] I don't mean it in uh, you know, like it's a bad thing, or necessarily a good thing, it's just...

Here, European, again, comes to stand for whiteness and is contrasted, this time, to Italians. Emerson talks about race as skin tone—as if all white people have literally white skin. As an Italian-American, Emerson by his own definition, and arguably by his own history, is not white; however by today's most common racial categories, he appears to be white and indeed is readily recognized as such by strangers. The apparent cleavage between how Emerson identifies himself, and how others would likely see him, speaks both to the invisibility of his own white privilege and to the historical roots of Italians in the United States.

The ability to recognize a person as white relies on assumed and shared cultural knowledge that articulates historical processes of pseudo-scientific frameworks that have been enforced through legal, social, and economic mechanisms. In the early nineteenth century, Italian, Irish, and Polish immigrants faced exclusion in terms of housing and employment because they occupied, at best, an ambiguous position in relation to whiteness (Roediger 1994, 2002). Early legal decisions and so-called scientific evidence intertwined with popular notions of race to create a nation based on white supremacy.[11] As a result, despite pervasive racialized discrimination, Italian, Irish, and Polish immigrants did not face anti-miscegenation laws, or legal restrictions on land ownership, citizenship, and immigration—as did Chinese, Filipino, and Japanese immigrants. Nor did Italian, Irish, and Polish immigrants experience the horrors of conquest and enslavement, as did Mexicans, Africans, and Native Americans. In short, Italian, Irish, and Polish immigrants were not included in the *institutionalization* of racial categories that were produced through conquest, enslavement, as well as through the refusal of citizenship, legal protection, and voting rights (cf., Omi and Winant 1994). So while stories of discrimination linger in family and community histories, today Italians are legally white, although socially they may inhabit a more marginal space that is somewhat "off-white."

The racializing history of conquest also enables nationality to mark people, who have visibly white skin tone, as "not white" (cf., López 1996; Omi 1994; Vidal-Ortiz 2004). For instance, if Mexicans may be white by contemporary standards of skin color, they are not white by legal or dominant discursive standards in the United States. Notions of race as color and nationality collide for people who may be recognized as white based on appearance but who come from a nationality that is "not white." In academia, analytic distinctions between race and ethnicity generally speak to these contradictions. However, in my interviews, people consistently referred to Italians as an ethnic group, but to Mexicans as a *racial* group. The people I interviewed only talked about *ethnicity* when referring to people whose countries of origin were already commonly understood as white—hence the expression "ethnic whites," which has no counterpart. Commonsense naturalizes complex historical productions of power through articulations of racialization that appear to be self-evident; yet the production of race continues to slide in ways that are fraught with contradictions. The following excerpt, in which Cuauhtemoc talked about his experience with race as a child, is an exemplar of how the production of race slides:

> *Cuauhtemoc:* And so when I would go to Mexico to visit my grandparents and family and cousins. Uhm, you know, they—they kinda—it bothered them a little bit that I didn't know how to speak Spanish. I understood everything, but I couldn't speak it so they were like "oh here comes the pinche pocho again, the guy from the Norte," you know, up north. You know, dadadada doesn't know how to speak Spanish. They were like "you're not Mexican you're a little white boy."
>
> *Celine-Marie:* Ouch.
>
> *Cuauhtemoc:* Yeah, but when I would come back home—I considered the States my home—I would get criticized uh, you know, by Anglo people "oh look at this Mexican kid." So being born here and being a Latino, being a Mexican—of Mexican heritage—it was really hard. It was really confusing. So I was really, really confused. I didn't know who I was or really—I knew who my parents were and I knew what the United States was, but who was **I**?

Cuauhtemoc was born in the United States to Mexican parents who worked in the agricultural fields of California. In this excerpt, it becomes clear that his parental heritage, cultural heritage, language, and skin color were not enough to secure a stable identity for him.

While his family in Mexico characterized him as white because he did not speak Spanish (and perhaps because he lived in the United States), in the United States, people characterized him as Mexican. In Mexico, language, as a marker of nationality, overrode color as a marker of race; in the United States, color and parental heritage overrode language. How people characterized Cuauhtemoc's racial identity slipped between white and Mexican depending on the hegemonic racial discourse of where he was at the time—and the racial identity of the people making the characterization.[12] Yet this slippage was never kind or innocent. Cuauhtemoc lives in the liminal space of Anzaldúa's (1987, 37) Atzlan: "A borderland is a vague and undetermined place created by the emotional residue of an unnatural boundary." Within the borderland of Mexican immigration and Chicana/o discourse, the term *pocho* (half-breed) is understood to target "gringo-ized Mexicans" who live in the United States (Chabram-Dernersesian 1997).

> In his seminal essay on the topic, "Pochos, the Different Mexicans," Arturo Madrid-Barela proposes that "it [pocho] was not an affectionate apodo (nickname). To be a pocho was only slightly worse than being a pinche gringo....Our accommodations to American society were traiciones (betrayals) in their eyes, era agringarse" (it was to become white). (cited in Chabram-Dernersesian 1997, 145).

In this sense, the slur, *pocho,* functions as a disciplinary mechanism that negotiates contemporary social, economic, and national interests. If Cuauhtemoc's family teased him harshly ("Oh here comes the pinche pocho again, the guy from the Norte." And "you're a little white boy"), in the United States, Cuauhtemoc understood being called "Mexican" as an indictment. ("I would get criticized uh, you know, by Anglo people 'oh look at this Mexican kid.'") The ability of nationality to stand-in for racial categories makes it possible for the characterization "Mexican" to function as *a racial slur in itself.* This left Cuauhtemoc with little room to claim with pride any sense of a collective identity—racial or national. As a child, he struggled to make his identity reliably recognizable within and across social, political, and historical fields. Cuauhtemoc framed his struggle over identity in terms of language, nationality, and color. The difficulties of racial categorization and identity emerge again as Cuauhtemoc talks about himself ("So being born here and being a Latino, being a Mexican—of Mexican heritage").

In Cuauhtemoc's talk about his childhood are sesonances of the historically shaped communities, alliances, oppositions, appropriations, and exploitations through which race was, and is, produced. The desire to mark "difference" is an apparatus of knowledge/power that fixes identity. However, race is an unstable complex of meanings, consistently anchored to the enunciative power of those who are marking "difference." Racial identity may be an intensely personal matter but race categorization is a profoundly social and political process. Painful conflicts between personal and social race categorizations were most evident in my interviews with Latinos. To the extent that racial identities are shaped by categorizations based on social histories, no one is ever entirely in control of their racial identity. And, to the extent that such processes shape our identities, all identity is a form of "passing"— the performance of an internalized identification.[13]

Commonsense naturalizes complex historical productions of power through articulations of racialization that appear to be self-evident. Although commonsense leads us to expect race to be visually recognizable, it also leads us to accept that race can be a matter of nationality. While commonsense tells us we can identify race based on skin color, the same skin tones can be racialized differently. And, if commonsense reifies race as a life-long identity, it is a reification subject to change and negotiation for many. The incoherence of race as a social category has led scholars (cf., Gilroy 2000) to envision a utopian "end of race" as the illogical basis of race is exposed. However, the usefulness of race has never depended on logic. In daily life, it appears that talk about race is part of a "debased discourse [that] doesn't care whether the terms of 'othering' are logical or not" (Lubiano 1992, 342). However, I want to argue these contradictions are both *fundamental* to the stability of race, and *less contradictory* than they might seem.

In analyses of race that focus *only* on local contexts of talk and interaction, the various ways of conceptualizing race as culture, color, blood, and nation can appear to be incongruous, if not contradictory. At the same time, theoretical analyses of discourse often occlude the daily practices through which people participate in producing the appearance of race and normalizing its effects. Because commonsense knowledge links the local production of meanings to the cultural production of knowledge, it provides a key focal point for examining the dialogical relationship between the apparent agency of local practices and the efficacy of cultural discourse.

Consider, for instance, that discursive formations are composed not only of chains of inference but also of points of contradiction or what Foucault (1972) called points of diffraction. Apparent incompatibilities constitute the raw materials of the discursive formation—as points of dispersion, they expand base of the discursive formation. This is the insidiousness of race. People who would never talk about race as a biological phenomenon are quite comfortable characterizing race as culture —something apparently quite different from biology. Yet it is the very way that older notions of biological races work through related discourses of nation that enables people to talk about race as culture. Cultural essentialism comes to replace biological essentialism.

Across interviews, newspapers, and television, commonsense produced race as an inherently meaningful category whose relevance did not need to be explained, or even agreed upon, in local contexts. Because knowledge/power always exceeds the immediate moment, it must be understood by how it travels through points of dispersion in discursive formations. The apparent contradictions regarding the meaning of race are the very components through which the discursive formation of race is stabilized. The seeming incoherence (i.e., points of diffraction) of racial discourse provides important alternatives which function as linkage points of systemization and enable race to travel, emerging differently in particular times and places, while still being rooted to the original discriminatory hierarchy. In themselves, each point of diffraction can generate more discursive formations, each with possible new points of incompatibility (Foucault 1972). In this sense, discursive formations function much like rhizomes linking together different manifestations of a central plant (Derrida 1976). The meaning of race can be constantly "differed" through points of diffraction and through chains of inference. Race does not need to have some fixed meaning in order to endure. Rather, it endures because the symbolic power of raced bodies always exceeds rational demands for coherence. Because race has no inherent meaning that stands apart from relations of power, the ways in which race can be produced as meaningful are not only contradictory but nearly unlimited; race is such a broad discursive formation that the criteria of racial characterizations can be discredited and remade without challenging the fundamental architecture of power that we call race. The apparent incoherence of race is not its death knell; rather it is evidence of how transformations in discourse can work to stabilize the central discursive formation. It also demonstrates the importance of studying language through *both* the local contexts of talk and the cultural contexts of discourse.

Talk and Discourse: A Study of Contexts and Power

The ability for race to appear to be self-evident, a matter of commonsense, speaks to how the history and the politics of race remain deeply submerged, yet easily readable in daily life. The invisible force of power becomes legible at the sites where discursive practices transform history into readable spaces. Commonsense secures the social, historical, political, and economic spaces that give race its materiality by producing race as a matter that requires no thought—which leads people to believe they simply *see* race. This imposition of obviousness renders *routine* decisions about racial characterizations unnecessary. To be "raced" is to be subjected to a set of regulations that formulate one's place in society (past, present, and future). In this sense, race is never benign; it is a measure of social distances between people. Even if these distances carry no fixed meaning, the fact that such distances continue to be both marked and intelligible is testimony to the power of language to preserve histories. The moral ontology of race resides within the very ability to recognize racial difference, regardless of the ground on which difference is named.

It is impossible to separate the apparent presence of race from the historical production of race—however it is very easy, particularly in studies of the local context of talk, to *misread* the ways in which submerged cultural discourses transform, travel, and emerge at various places and times. This is what makes conceptions of race appear to be incoherent and contradictory. Hence, the politics of difference requires a return to the analytical tensions between material and discursive analyses of race to rethink ways to confront the effects of racism without reifying race. The materiality of lived experience gives rise to identity-based politics, which regard "difference" in pragmatic terms of social experience, opportunity, status, language, and culture. Identity-based politics assume an essentialism that can be historical, cultural, or biological. Theories of intersectionality complicate and challenge aspects of this essentialism but cannot escape its burden because they remain tethered to same epistemology of the subject. Theories of social construction and essentialism do not exist in opposition to each other; rather, biological essentialism is rearticulated through social constructions based on culture and history. Yet, to argue for alliances based on shared interests (cf., Guinier and Torres 2003) belies the fact that interests are formed in relationship to subject positions. Consequently, interest and identity come "to seem interchangeable (as in "women's issues" or "the black agenda"). In such cases, the interest stands in for the identity in public discourse, and the latter appears not as an active and *interactive* agent of political life, but as an entrenched and inert position" (Adams 2002, 9).

Poststructural discourse analysis offers an understanding of difference as strategic and positional, and of identity as mobile and performative. Within this analytical frame, a social justice agenda seeks to disrupt the vernacular moral order by rupturing the broad binaries of racial categories, through which race is reproduced, in order to disrupt the repetition of race and racism. The effects of race are real, but it is a mistake to locate the materiality of race in bodies. As soon as one questions the material unity of race, one is left not with bodies that have experiences but with a complex field of discourses rooted to relations of appropriation and exploitation. Discourses are not imaginary relations; they inscribe and are inscribed by the materiality of social, institutional, and cultural practices. The discourse of commonsense produces the apparently self-evident nature of race that comes to symbolize not only a history but also a vision of power.

The conundrum is this: collective interests of racialized groups are both real and important, but equality is impossible if we continue to reify the architecture of race through which inequality is produced. I want to make an argument for alliances through a politics of disindentification that subverts hegemonic power by making visible what hegemonic discourse conceals. I am not suggesting a utopian promise but a strategic enterprise that calls for exposing the production of race on a daily level by confronting what appears to be obvious—learning to see that which commonsense actively works to conceal.

The power of commonsense about race is broadly cultural and discursive even as it is locally produced, transformed, and challenged through specific practices. At the same time, however, it would be a mistake to attribute the vast power of language exclusively to discourse. It is in local contexts and local practices that discourses gain their materiality. And, it is in local contexts, in the "everydayness" of living, that the possibility of agency and the potential for change exists. If we accept that all knowledge is historically situated, we must question the adequacy of social theories and movements of the 1960s for engaging the issues and troubles of today. As we witness the erosion of civil rights, an increase in poverty, and the strategic political appointments including Alberto Gonzales, Condoleeza Rice, Elaine Chao, and Janice Rogers Brown, the echo "my color, but not my kind" is a reverberating disavowal of the Bush administration's agenda. It is a disavowal that demands the creation of a different sort of social justice movement. Throughout this book I continue to develop analyses that raise such possibilities by bridging local and cultural contexts through analyses of commonsense knowledge.

3

ALL THE RIGHT STUFF
GENDER AND SEXUALITY

In the late 1960s, audiences in the United States laughed each week as Goldie Hawn appeared as a "dumb blond" on *Rowan and Martin's Laugh In* and danced in a bikini, her body painted with multicolor images, slogans, and jokes. If Hawn could be read as a symbol of the "liberated woman" who inhabited the sexual revolution, on the streets, less ambiguous symbols of revolution held sway. The women's liberation movement roiled with ground-swelling activism and promised a vision of women's future as both sexually self-determined and politically empowered. The sacrifices made by millions of women provided considerable gains to subsequent generations of women including, access to credit in their own names, equal opportunity legislation for employment and education, Title IX, abortion rights, access to reproductive health care, as well as protections and support for rape victims and battered women.

[In the ferment of the era, the term "gender" emerged, creating a key shift in public discourse that proved to be a powerful tool in feminist arguments for equality.] If Simone de Beauvoir gave the world some understanding of what it meant to "become" a woman, the term "gender" provided a discursive frame for advancing that understanding. Gender, as culturally constructed masculinity/femininity, was juxtaposed against the biological attribute of sex (Stoller 1968; Oakley 1972).

The delineation between culture and nature, implicit in the gender/sex paradigm, became part of an enduring legacy—particularly to ensuing scholarship. Research on gender flourished in diverse analytical directions. For example, socialist feminism (Acker 1973; Eisenstein 1990; Hartmann 1982; Mies 1986; Mitchell 1971) locates the oppression of women in the intersection of capitalism and patriarchy; while, radical feminism (Brownmiller 1976; Bunch 1987; Daly 1978; Dworkin 1974) argues that the root of women's oppression was patriarchy. Various inflections of standpoint feminisms (Collins 1993; Hartsock 1987) assert that women's social location is produced through multiple relations of oppression, and as a result of their social locations, women have situated knowledge that should in itself be the topic of study. And, multiracial (also called intersectional) feminisms (Zinn 1979; Dill 1992; Glenn 1985, 2002) explore how the intersections of race, class, and gender affect the daily lives of women. Despite significant differences across these fields of study, all of this research and theory focuses analytically on the social construction of gendered identities and the attendant inequalities produced through social structures and/or social interactions.

By contrast, scholars concerned with issues of sex and sexuality challenged the binaries (gender/sex, male/female, culture/nature) on which gender scholarship was premised. In ethnomethodology, Garfinkel's (1967) early work on sex status as a social achievement challenged the naturalness of sex, as did Kessler and McKenna's (1978) study of sex/gender attribution, and West's (Fenstermaker, West, and Zimmerman 1991; West and Zimmerman 1987) work on sex and sex categories.[1] Ethnomethodological research on sex categories became central to later research on transsexual (Bornstien 1994; Shapiro 1991) and transgendered (Bullough 2001; Denny 1998; Kessler 2001) identities. At a minimum, studies of sex and sexuality challenge notions of biological sexualities and dimorphic sex categories. More fundamentally, challenges to the sex/gender binary were produced through changing epistemologies of subjectivity.

Foucault's (1978) genealogy of sex and sexuality provided a powerful resource for scholars concerned with the oppression of lesbian, gay, bisexual, and transgendered people, and his analytical strategies became fundamental to a variety of feminist, queer and poststructural/postmodern research (Butler 1990; Butler 1993; Fraser and Nicholson 1996; Grosz 1990).[2] Generally, the deconstructive strategies deployed by scholars of sex and sexuality helped to denaturalize heteronormativity and bring the politics of gendered sexuality into sharp relief (cf., Butler 1997b; Fuss 1989; Fuss 1991; Garber 1992; Sedgwick 1990; Seidman 1997a).

Despite brilliant scholarship with rich crosscurrents, at the start of the twenty-first century, commonsense knowledge regarding sex, sexuality, and gender that fuels public discourse appears to be both less nuanced and less in sync with academic knowledge than it was forty years ago. For example, I found that commonsense knowledge still holds gender to be simply the nature of persons. Further, I found that across all interviews, newspaper articles, and television shows everyone—except transgendered interviewees—appeared to conflate gender and sex.[3] Indeed, commonsense knowledge regarding the self-evident nature of gender made any questions that I asked about the *meaning* of gender an exercise in breaching (cf., Garfinkel 1967).[4] In addition, the heterosexual people I interviewed consistently talked about gender in ways that conflated— not only sex and gender—but also gender and sexuality.

In this chapter, I revisit gender, sex, and sexuality by examining commonsense knowledge. If this project seems to be turning back the feminist clock on well-established fields, consider that many of the rights that women fought so hard to secure seem less certain than they once did. The U.S. government refused to pass an equal rights amendment and legislation that was enacted has been sidestepped. Women have yet to achieve pay equity: "according to the most recent Census Bureau statistics, the average woman working full-time, year-round, earns just 76¢ for every $1.00 earned by the average man; many women of color fare even worse, with African American women making 66¢ on the dollar and Latinas making only 55¢" (cited in The National Committee on Pay Equity 2005). Women increasingly suffer from eating disorders and sexual assaults. In addition, significant reproductive rights are being rolled back. As of this writing, pharmacies in eleven states have obtained the legal right to refuse to dispense physician prescribed birth control to single women. At the same time, research data on the status of women is being removed from government Web sites.

Contemporary lesbian, gay, bisexual, and transgendered (LGBT) movements arose not only from the Stonewall riots but also from a lineage of protest initiated by the civil rights movement and carried forward, in part, through the women's liberation movement. Despite the rich complexity and success of these movements, social and economic gains for LGBT people are both limited and at risk. In 2004 alone there were nearly three hundred LGBT-related bills introduced in state capitols; 92 percent were intended to restrict marriage and other civil rights (HRC 2005). Only seventeen states prohibit discrimination against lesbian and gay persons in employment and housing; seven states protect public employees from employment discrimination; five states prohibit discrimination based on gender identity; twelve states plus the District of Columbia offer domestic partner benefits (Lambda 2005). Members of LGBT communities in general, and transgendered people in particular, face brutal physical violence with depressing regularity.

If sex/sexuality and gender are well-established fields in academia, social and political life seem to call for new forms of strategic engagements. How might revisiting commonsense notions of gender, sex, and sexuality provide insights into strategies for advancing social theory and social change? What cultural assumptions about gender, sex, and sexuality give shape and meaning to contemporary social life?

Through the Looking Glass

As one might expect, distinctions between sex and gender rarely appeared in interviews or media. By and large, commonsense renders distinctions between sex and gender irrelevant—something that just never comes up—and enables sex and gender to operate as synonyms. What work does this accomplish? What effects does this production secure? To answer these questions I analyze those few excerpts in interviews and media where sex and gender were not collapsed.

In interviews, the only people I talked with who did *not* conflate gender and sex were Ashley Worthington and Emerson Piscopo. Significantly, Ashley and Emerson also were the only transgendered people I interviewed. In the following excerpt of Ashley's interview, the number of stops, starts, and stammers might make reading difficult; however, these are important illustrations of how Ashley struggles to formulate her ideas, despite her initial confidence about her knowledge regarding gender. Ashley Worthington, had just finished talking about the possibility of having a person of color in the presidency, when I asked her what gender meant to her.

Ashley:	Oh this is something I have a LOT more ready answer for, I think. Gender means um [pause] maybe I don't [laughs]. Um gender has a lot more to do with, like I think it's like, I've been talking a lot with my friend Michele about this stuff as well. I think that it has a lot more of a …uh…it has a lot more fundamental meaning I think to a lot of …to…to…everybody because we all HAVE these gender identities that we all construct and gender is essentially…uh cultural behaviors that we take on which are stratified along our perceived sex.
Celine-Marie:	Uh-huh, uh-huh.
Ashley:	Would you mind if I went potty real quick?

One of the inherent problems with direct questions in interviews is that interviewees often feel the need to have a "ready answer." This is not a topic that Ashley initiated. This excerpt begins with Ashley referring back to our earlier conversation about race and reflects her greater comfort level talking about gender—a common feature of my conversations with white women. Ashley does not invoke grammars of nature and self-evidence but refers to our earlier discussion of race. Here, gender gains importance as a universal category framed *against* race, which Ashley refers to as a limited category, something not everyone has; indeed, Ashley talks as if she has a gender but not a race.[5] It is not surprising then that Ashley talks about gender as more important (more fundamental) than race because it is a characteristic of all people.

Ashley also talks about gender like a house one can build and inhabit ("we all HAVE these gender identities that we all construct"). Certainly, one could argue that Ashley—who refers to herself as a transgendered woman—now inhabits a gender identity that she could be said to have constructed for herself. Later in the interview when talking about her childhood, Ashley said: "Pretty much I determined from a very early age that I wasn't, I wasn't a boy. And like I KNEW that. [...] It was difficult to like make other people SEE that." Ashley explains that as a child, she was perceived to be a boy *physically*, when in fact she was really a girl, psychically. Hence, it seems that when Ashley resists being classified by *perceived* sex, she embraces a sex that is *not* perceived—it is *this* sex, which Ashley, as a transgendered woman, has been working to bring to the surface of her life.

Ashely's experience ruptures hegemonic commonsense knowledge about gender and sets her apart from her family and community. To the extent that commonsense holds the world to be self-evident and uncomplicated, when people provide information that *contradicts* commonsense knowledge, listeners tend to question either the adequacy of the person or of the adequacy of the account (Pollner 1987). In the case of transgendered persons, it is not only a matter of providing *information* that contradicts commonsense, one's very being is a living contradiction. Evidence of how transgendered women and men consistently find their adequacy as humans judged as suspect, can be found in the many ways they are deprived of full civil rights and targeted for malicious hate crimes.

Emerson Piscopo also described an inner self that conflicted with his "perceived sex." Born as a biological female, Emerson explained: "Spiritually, I feel like a man." When we met, Emerson had undergone surgery and was beginning hormone therapy to support his transition from female to male. For Ashley and Emerson, gender did not "naturally" evolve from their sex; they each experienced sex and gender as contradictory, not complementary.

Emerson Piscopo, like Ashley Worthington, changed his body to match an inner sense of self. Despite their experiences of a disjunction between sex and gender, their behaviors underscore a very deep cultural belief that sex is *naturally* gendered—that there *should be* a one-to-one correspondence between sex and gender (cf., Butler 1990; Garfinkel 1967; Kessler and McKenna 1978). Hegemonic discourse on gender produces both the possibility and the terms of being *trans*-gendered. Even as the experiences of Emerson and Ashley rupture hegemonic commonsense, they must draw from the culturally specific discourses to understand and interpret their experiences. This gives rise to the sense of being in the wrong body (e.g., being a woman but having a penis).

Both Emerson and Ashley participated in hormone therapy to change their physical appearances and both were considering further surgical possibilities to bring their physical sex characteristics in line with their conception of inner selves. Each had to learn to achieve femaleness and maleness, respectively, through practical actions and everyday activities. Individuals *do gender* by orienting their actions in relation to hegemonic conceptions of appropriate behavior for "women" and "men." [6] In any interaction, we may be held accountable to others for how we do gender; that is, we may be held responsible for our behavior *as* women or *as* men (Fenstermaker, West, and Zimmerman 1991; West and Fenstermaker 1995; West and Zimmerman 1987). For example, consider that just after Ashley's allusion to "our perceived sex," in the previous excerpt, she asks: "Would you mind if I went potty real quick?" Here, Ashley "does gender" by the way she raises a need for a break in the interview. [7]

Transgressive practices must always, to some extent, reinforce the hegemonic discourses they seek to transcend, because they are produced within the same terms of intelligibility (cf., Butler 1990; Foucault 1978). Ashley and Emerson, as a transgendered woman and man, disrupt cultural knowledge about gender as a life-long, one-to-one correspondence with sex, *and* they also reinscribe the sex/gender binary required to regulate heterosexuality.

Although changing genders is a transgressive practice, it is one motivated by a powerful, and coerced, *identification with* hegemonic discourses of gender and sex. It is this identification that reinscribes that which it appears to resist. "The highest purpose of the transsexual is to erase himself/herself, to fade into the 'normal' population as soon as possible" (Stone 1998, 328). While this is often the case, many transgendered persons refuse such complete assimilation; for others, the ability to "fade into the 'normal' population," is just not completely possible. Their visibility as being transgendered, like the presence of butch women and queenly men, fractures the misnomer of a one-to-one correspondence between sex and gender and places them at enormous risk, not only of discrimination in housing and employment but of deadly physical assault.

Gender practices that openly break the one-to-one correspondence with sex and gender strategically transfigure and negotiate cultural power/knowledge; they are a *dis-identification* with hegemonic practices (cf., Muñoz 1998; Pêcheux 1994). Disidentification is still produced through terms set by hegemonic gender discourse, but it does not necessarily reinscribe normative conceptions of sex/gender/sexuality—in this sense, *disidentification ruptures commonsense knowledge through the refusal of the hegemonic terms of accountability.* Because hegemonic gender produces the misnomer of a preexisting sex and sexuality, "butch women" are misunderstood as attempting to be copies of men, imitations of heteronormativity; rather, they should be understood evidence of multiple genders for each sex (Butler 1990). Butch women in general and butch lesbians in particular, do not replicate masculinity so much as they constitute another way of being gendered. Gender, in this sense, no longer produces the misnomer of a preexisting sex and sexuality. The lived reality of a polymorphic psyche is necessarily found in acts of resistance against being interpolated as either a man or woman—acts that insist on a multiplicity of ways of being gendered. Benjamin (1995) argues that if gender is oriented to the pull of opposite poles, then these poles are not masculinity and femininity. "Rather, gender dimorphism itself represents only one pole, the other pole being the polymorphism of the psyche" (Benjamin 1995, 120).

In fifteen years of newspaper articles about homelessness, I found no references to transgendered or transsexual persons, and the apparent need for distinctions between sex and gender never arose. While television characters of ambiguous gender have appeared as the source of comedy in the past (e.g., the character Pat in *Saturday Night Live* skits), out of the nine shows and three genres that I studied, I found only two shows that included segments in which people's appearances contradicted the commonsense knowledge that sex and gender have a one-to-one correspondence—both were news magazines.

While news magazines appear to produce reality as a preexisting, material world that can be known through rational knowledge, by necessity, they produce the world as a spectacle—a dramatic display that renders the everyday remarkable (cf., Cowie 1999). In news magazines, as in documentary film, events are interesting because they stand—or are made to stand—apart from ordinary life (cf., Gaines 1999). Indeed *20/20*'s "news" coverage of transsexual women was evidence of just such a process.

The *20/20* segment entitled "The Eunuchs of India" (aired October 14, 1999) opened with reporter Anderson Cooper, an apparently white man in jeans and a casual shirt, walking down a street in New Delhi amidst women in brightly colored saris and scarves, a few men wearing Indian clothing, and several small children. At first the street appears to be filled with a random mix of people going about their lives, yet, on second glance, they clearly are an orchestrated presence. The people stop and advance toward the camera as a group synchronized with Cooper's movements.[8] As he talks, they crowd around him, despite the obvious presence of open space around this group. As Cooper and the small crowd walk toward the camera, the view narrows and the group pulls more tightly around Cooper. Although no one in the group is talking or playing music, a loud sound track overlays this segment and includes ambient street noise, people talking, singing, and drumming. The sound and camera create a noisy, congested feeling; it is difficult to hear Cooper over the sound track as he opens the news segment:

> I've come here to India to discover the secrets of the eunuchs—a mysterious [unclear] society whose members are seen as neither male nor female. I've heard eunuchs have special powers. That they search out newborn babies demanding cash from their parents or they'll curse the child. I've heard young boys are kidnapped, castrated, and turned into prostitutes. I've been told no outsider can ever learn the truth about the eunuchs. No outsider can understand this strange tradition, in this place where ...
>
> [*Cooper pauses as if searching for a word. He opens his arms and looks to the left with a small grimace, then turns toward the camera and continues.*]
>
> nothing is as it seems.

Cooper distances himself from the very information that he reports by saying he has "heard" and "been told" about "the special powers" and the "curse[s]" of eunuchs. Cooper does *not* refer to people who are neither male nor female. Rather, he reports that eunuchs "are *seen* as neither male nor female." His distinction emphasizes that even if some people believe in "special powers," no one believes that people exist who actually are "neither male nor female." In addition, Cooper's characterization underscores sex categorization as visual activity—and, as a process that may be wrong. Notably, Cooper refers to the subjects of his news segment as eunuchs, despite a later admission that he is uncertain which people might be "eunuchs" and which might be "homosexuals."

The crowding and noise that are central to the opening scene offer an example of how television produces meaning, not by representing reality through talk and interaction, but through a particular grammar of representation that has technical, narrative, and discursive aspects (cf., Gray 1995a, b). These strategies converge to produce and reproduce discourses about India as well as about gender. The opening sequence of Cooper's story orchestrates text, sound, and camera work to produce strangeness and chaos with respect to the eunuchs in particular, and also, with respect to India in general. The strangeness of India and of the people "seen as neither male nor female" come together as Cooper says, "No outsider can understand this strange tradition, in this place where..." Cooper pauses and glances around. As he returns his gaze to the camera, his slight grimace suggests incomprehension, perhaps disdain—and then he finishes his sentence: "nothing is as it seems." The pause, itself full of meanings, heightens the dramatic effect of Cooper's pronouncement that "nothing is as it seems." Everyone and everything he surveys becomes an object of suspicion. The technical aspects of the opening sequence generate obtrusive noise and chaos to produce both "people who appear to be neither men nor women" and India as a whole, as incomprehensibly strange and inherently suspicious. Cooper's grimaced assessment that "nothing is as it seems" is not a happy one.

Themes of gender ambiguity and xenophobia thread together, articulating through each other in this segment. For instance, the camera shows a "eunuch," dressed in a beautiful sari, pick through a pile of squash and walk away with a single squash without paying as the vendor watches. As if we are witnessing an unorchestrated event, Cooper narrates this scene through a voice over and describes how eunuchs are free to steal because people fear their curse. Cooper then interviews an Indian journalist "who has researched eunuchs" and who tells Cooper: "For the vendor this is very auspicious, he will think that he will have a good sale because he gave a gift to somebody who is a condemned lot." While the reporter explains that this exchange has a particular meaning within a predominantly Hindu culture, Cooper immediately reframes the religious aspects of giving a "a gift to somebody who is a condemned lot" for an American audience by describing it as "extortion" based on "superstition."

The "eunuchs" look and dress like women and the local journalist consistently refer to each of them as "she." By contrast, Cooper consistently refers to each of the "eunuchs" as "he"—thereby asserting a fundamental male-ness beneath appearances. For Cooper, the *reported* presence of a penis establishes sex categorization as a male despite the powerful visual presence of women. In the United States, commonsense leads people to assume that gender has a one-to-one correspondence with sex—that gender is a cultural proxy for biological sex (Garfinkel 1967). In this circumstance, commonsense is breached and Cooper's use of "he" functions as an effort to make the disjuncture between sex and gender visible, and thereby render it in some way potentially accountable. While an ethnomethodological understanding of accountable activities depends upon relevant norms, I want to avoid the prescriptive force of social expectations associated with norms and instead assert an understanding of accountability that is linked to what Foucault called the "political anatomy" of details (Foucault 1977, 139). That is to say, a detailed political investment in the body is enacted through a "micro-physics of power," in which small acts and subtle gestures, even the smallest details, become a form of an account that constitutes a meaningful presence—and as such, can be made potentially accountable to others. By linking the concept of accountability to that of a political anatomy of detail, local productions of appearance, demeanor, and interaction can be better understood as politicized expressions of knowledge/power.

Despite Cooper's consistent use of "he," in this segment, when *20/20* arrives at the home of a group of "eunuchs," Cooper, standing in the doorway, turns to the camera and says: "These eunuchs here are viewed as neither man nor woman. I'm not exactly sure what [pause] to refer to them as—whether I should say he or she." Cooper winces as he talks and repeatedly looks down and away from the camera, as if embarrassed. If Cooper's admitted confusion contradicts his insistence on referring to "eunuchs" as "he," it also promises some impending clarification.

A "eunuch" comes to the front door and extends her hand to Cooper and to the person behind the camera. As if this moment of arrival were an accident, Cooper then confesses: "I have to say I feel awkward because they just got out of the shower and are putting on makeup." The camera then pans to "eunuchs" putting on bras, applying makeup, and brushing their hair. Cooper's confession makes it possible to read the voyeuristic scan of the camera as an exhibitionist tendency of the "eunuchs." Since we are forced, by accident, to witness this moment, we are absolved of having any interest in observing the partially clothed bodies of "eunuchs," of the desire to see what is really beneath the clothes and makeup.

Throughout the segment Cooper's interest focuses on a "eunuch" who, by American standards, appears to be a conventionally beautiful woman. In a voice over, that distances Cooper from the assessment he animates, Cooper reports that her breasts are natural as she poses for the camera. Cooper then appears facing the camera and says, "It is true that after castration a man's body can become somewhat feminine because it doesn't produce testosterone. Let's just leave it one of those eunuch secrets." Cooper, in the face of the physical evidence he sought, declines to investigate the very "secrets" he came to uncover ("I've come here to India to discover the secrets of the eunuchs"). Cooper closes the segment:

> I left them as I found them, living in their own world. Their glorious past long since vanished but their resilience continuing in the chaos and confusion, the myth and mystery, of India.

His wistful colonialist posture ("I left them as I found them, living in their own world") makes it possible to understand his closing remarks about "them" as being about Indians as well as eunuchs. In this *20/20* segment, the meaning of ambiguously sexed/gendered persons was produced through another discourse of strangeness and marginality: the colonial subject. The episode not only reinforces commonsense knowledge that all people are—or *should be*—distinctly women or men, the representations of ambiguous gender cannot be separated from a romantically xenophobic gaze ("the chaos and confusion, the myth and mystery, of India"). In this segment, gender, race, sexuality, class, and nationality are not competing or oppositional forces but rather are discourses that articulate through each other. *The unmarked character of one becomes the condition of articulation of the other* (Butler 1999, 168). In this complex configuration of historically-shaped relations of domination, subjectivity is the terrain of multiple struggles. Consequently, the mutual constitution of gender, race, sexuality, class, and nationality is necessarily characterized by the unevenness of subordination.

Colonial discourses, which are necessarily, and fundamentally, racist and xenophobic, saturate this particular example. Yet, in order to consider the xenophobia, racism, and colonialism of this clip, one must follow the trace of language beyond the boundaries of the immediate context—to examine how words have been marked by the politics of their use (cf., de Certeau 1984). This requires a shift from an analysis of *talk* to an analysis of *discourse*, a shift from the daily practices that constitute meaning to the conceptual practices that constitute knowledge. Poststructural discourse analysis offers, not a history of events but rather, a genealogy that attempts to make visible the conditions of emergence. For instance, a racist slur could not be a slur if it was not a repetition—a "citation" of itself—that produces a relationship to an "historically transmitted community" of racists (Butler 1997a). We know the force and offensiveness of slurs only because of how they have been used in the past (Butler 1997a). In this sense, an entire history and culture is invoked in the speech of one person. The meanings of gender—that appear to be self-evident—are (re)produced and resisted in local contexts *through* linkages to discursive formations regarding race and colonialism as well as through discourses about gender and sex. By examining what passes as commonsense, it becomes possible to explore the processes through which social knowledge becomes self-evident and through which relations of power are hidden.

Gender and Sexuality

A rich body of scholarship reveals the apparently natural one-to-one correspondence between sex and gender as the effect of regulatory practices required by compulsory heterosexuality (cf., Foucault 1978; Rich 1980; Butler 1990). And, indeed, across interviews, newspaper articles, and television shows commonsense knowledge about gender functioned to secure the presumption of heterosexuality. In this section, I explore a nuanced, and sometimes surprising, analysis of how this disciplinary mechanism functions. For example, the heterosexual people I interviewed all lacked a general facility for distinguishing between gender and *sexuality*—regardless of their educational background, race, or class.[9] Lana Jacobs talked about gender like this: "Gender is the difference [clears throat] it's the difference between our sexual orientation, the difference in our make up, there's men, there's women." It is not entirely clear if Lana is conflating gender and sexual orientation or, if she means "sex" when she says "sexual orientation." This blurring of terms, common among the heterosexuals I interviewed, reflects a lack of facility, if not a lack of familiarity, for talking about distinctions among sex, gender, and sexual orientation. Similarly, Cuauhtemoc commented on *gender* this way: "I guess, we're all wherever we are, you know, like I said, you know, some people are heterosexual some are this and some are that, it's not big deal to me."

Heterosexuals' tendency to conflate sexual orientation and gender also appeared as interviewees completed an interview form that had a blank requesting "sexual orientation." Many people were uncertain of how to respond to this part of the form. And, in this uncertainty, homophobia often emerged. Polard Parker, for instance, asked: "I like girls—is that what you mean?" He seemed genuinely embarrassed. As we sat at his kitchen table, Polard continued: "Well, if you weren't here, I'd write normal."[10] In the end, Polard did write "normal" for his sexual orientation. By contrast, Brownie Wu burst into laughter when she read "sexual orientation." "I've had some," she said. After we had finished laughing at her pun, Brownie continued to ponder what to write in the blank. The problem for Brownie was not whether to make an intimate revelation, but how to name the fact that she was married to a man—she asked, "what is the word for that?" Roberta Washington, perplexed by the blank on the interview form labeled "sexual orientation," looked at me and said, "I'm a girl." I explained what I had intended by sexual orientation to her. Roberta looked down at the form and then again at me and said, "I'm a girl." She then ended the discussion by writing "girl" in the blank. Roberta was unusual only in the way she took the situation in hand and put an end to the discussion. In interviews then, gender was produced as what Ingraham (1997) called "heterogender"—the appearance of heterosexuality produced through gender. That is, to be a woman or man is to be attracted to the opposite gender.[11] In this way, commonsense *should have* made it obvious to me that, because Roberta was a girl, she was sexually oriented toward men. To clarify and emphasize this point, in my research, across differences of gender, race, and class, heterosexual people talked about gender, not as an *indicator* of heterosexuality, but as sexuality itself.

The ability of gender to stand as evidence of sexual desire means that in daily life heterosexuality need not be named—it is an unmarked category in talk and representation. Concomitantly, nonhegemonic sexualities must be produced as marked categories. Consider that, in fifteen years of newspaper coverage about people who cannot afford housing, not one article mentioned gay, lesbian, or bisexual persons. One consequence is that it appears that either all people without housing are heterosexual or that sexuality is irrelevant to homelessness. The politics of this practice are not subtle; sexuality can be centrally relevant to people without housing, particularly in the case of teenagers who often are forced from their homes because of their sexuality. Yet here, as in Chapter 2, the erasures that produce privileged subject positions are not visible practices—the practices leave no quotes to analyze, no written text to which to point.

In order to explore the conflation of sexuality and gender that sustains heterosexuality, I examine how the heterosexual imaginary of primetime television shows produces sexual "difference."[12] Out of the nine shows that I studied, two shows (*The Practice* and *Judging Amy*) had episodes that included representations of lesbian, gay, or bisexual people or issues—both regarded apparently white, gay men. I examine both in this section and begin with the episode from *The Practice* (aired October 31, 1999). This episode interweaves two story lines revolving around the sexuality of two apparently white men: one about a middle-aged gay man, Joey, who murdered his lover, and the other about one of the firm's attorneys, Jimmy Berluti, a middle-aged heterosexual, being arrested for soliciting sex from a woman.

During the opening credits, the show establishes a drama in which Jimmy Berluti is arrested for soliciting sex. Berluti notices a young woman, for whom he previously had provided a pro bono defense, back at work, hooking on a street corner. He picks her up to discourage her entrepreneurial efforts, and goes so far as to lend her money to help her out. In gratitude, she offers him oral sex. Jimmy responds with flustered resistance, yet the woman persists, invoking the story of the little drummer boy who gave the Christ child the only gift he could offer, his song. After she unbuckles his belt and unzips his pants, a police officer knocks on the car window and arrests them both. Berluti stands falsely accused of a "bad" deed when, in fact, he is actually trying to do a "good" deed.

The show then cuts to stylishly modern living room. Attorneys Eleanor, Eugene, and Bobby are talking with Joey—who had called the lawyers to come to the scene where he had just murdered his lover. A butcher knife protrudes from the chest of an apparently white man collapsed on the couch. The camera is on Joey as he paces around the room contemplating what might happen when he calls the police:

Joey: Oh come on, look, look my lover is found dead. Obviously, I'm going to be considered a suspect. Just because I'm gay, every homophobe across America will think I did it. He's gay, he kills is practically a jingle.
    [*The camera cuts to Eugene.*]

Eugene: You DID do it.
    [*The camera returns to Joey, who is pacing.*]

Joey: All right the way I see it I have three options here. One, confess, go for manslaughter heat of passion.
    [*The camera cuts to Bobby who shakes his head.*]

Joey: Two, I plead insanity. Statistically I've got a shot there—a lot people think we're SICK anyway.
    [*The camera cuts to Eugene.*]

Eugene: I wouldn't go to the bank on that one.
    [*The camera returns to Joey who continues to pace.*]

Joey: Three, self-defense. My word against his. I mean how convincing can he be? He's dead. Or, I didn't do it at all.
    [*The camera cuts to Bobby who looks surprised.*]

Joey: I came home. I uh, I found him this way and my prints got on the knife when I tried to help him. Er, when I pulled it out.
           [Joey yanks the butcher knife from the dead man's chest. Then holding the knife and laughing, he turns toward the lawyers and the audience sees Joey from the vantage point of the lawyers.]

Joey: That was really stuck in there.
           [Joey looks at the knife with amazement. The camera changes to Joey's vantage point and we see the lawyers staring with horror and disgust. The camera turns back toward Joey; he smiles.]

Joey: What are your thoughts?

This scene plays on the irony that, as Joey considers what "every homophobe across America will think," he is guilty of the behavior he accuses homophobes of suspecting. Joey invokes the slur that he fulfills ("He's gay, he kills is practically a jingle."). Eugene, the only black man on the show, is the only person to confront Joey's invocation of homophobia. Eugene's response, "You DID do it," not only reinforces what the audience believes, having just heard Joey's confession, more importantly it frames Joey's consideration of homophobia as an unfair cry of injustice—the gay equivalent of "playing the race card." When Joey invokes homophobia a second time, "a lot of people think we're SICK anyway," Eugene again confronts him, "I wouldn't go to the bank on that one." Eugene, as a black man, seems to have special insight into Joey's false claim of injustice. If challenging "the race card" is the policing work of white racial hegemony, here we see Eugene extend such policing in the service of *heterosexual* hegemony. Throughout this scene, Joey's talk and behavior *reinforces* the initial slur by suggesting through his behavior that he *is* "sick" (e.g., forcefully yanking the knife from his lover's chest). His question ("What are your thoughts?") closes the scene and invites audience judgment as he holds the knife covered in blood.

The show cuts back to Jimmy Berluti recalling the details of his arrest to Lindsey and Rebecca, lawyers at the same firm, saying, "she didn't have any money so she wanted to play an instrument or something. I don't really remember. I'm completely innocent." Jimmy's apparent confusion is a means to constitute the innocence he proclaims. Yet his apparent innocence about sexuality comes at some risk, since it calls into question hegemonic notions of white, heterosexual, masculinity. Jimmy later retells the story for Bobby and the entire office in a way that attempts to recoup his masculinity, though not through virility, "I saw a client who is, you know, a lady of the evening. I gave her money cause she was completely broke. She started rubbing me and the police showed up. I've disgraced myself." Jimmy defines his disgrace by *her* behavior and through this can be seen to reconstitute his once-tarnished honor. Honor can do the work of restoring Jimmy's white masculinity, now that sexual prowess is unavailable. The show cuts back and forth between these developing story lines, countering Jimmy's heterosexuality and goodness with Joey's homosexuality and psychopathology.

The analytical point to be made here is not simply that the show presents Joey's criminality in the context of his homosexuality and presents Jimmy Berluti's claim to innocence and honor in the context of heterosexuality. Rather, *the naturalness of gender produces the innocence of heterosexuality.* To the extent that gender and heterosexuality are understood as a single expression of biology, they produce homosexuality (and necessarily, bisexuality) as culpable deviance.

While the show primarily establishes Joey's "gayness" through his talk about being gay and his talk about his lovers, it also anchors his sexuality through his interactions with women. Even though Eleanor is part of the three-person legal team defending Joey, he refuses to speak to her—at one point dismissing her from a conversation saying, "Why don't you go grab a pizza, jumbo?" Joey derides Eleanor's intelligence, sarcastically asking her, "Are you keeping up?" "Do you need to take notes?" He refers to a witness as "the old sack of a woman" and when arguing with the woman prosecuting attorney, sneers, "oh get real, skinny." All of Joey's interactions with women are openly hostile and no other characters confront his behavior.

The link between male homosexuality and misogyny produces gay sexuality as still being about women. That is, gay sexuality is still linked through gender to heterosexuality—but here, it is heterosexuality gone wrong. Homosexuality appears as the result of some failure in heterosexuality—and is reflective of Butler's (1997b) analysis of lesbianism as a failure of the "heterosexual machinery." While a detective in the episode makes homophobic remarks (he scoffs, "homosexuals" and asks, "another homo?"), the show's most vehement homophobic stereotypes are articulated through Joey, the only gay character to appear on *The Practice* in the 1999 season.

By the show's end, Jimmy Berluti's case was dropped, the record expunged, and his honor redeemed. He forgives the hooker, who had been coerced into framing him, and makes an effusive speech about the friendship of his coworkers, who have helped to clear his name. By contrast, by the show's end, Joey had dramatically and successfully manipulated everyone (the police, his lawyers, the prosecutor, the judge, and a lover) to his benefit. Under the terms of an immunity agreement established to prosecute one of Joey's lovers for the murder, he is able to confess to the murder and walk away completely free.

Joey smugly basks in having outwitted everyone. When asked by a reporter if he was "afraid of being sued," Joey replies, "All my assets are in off-shore trusts. Oh—they can have my Heisman!" This reference to news coverage of the O.J. Simpson murder trial makes explicit the symbolic connection to "the race card" suggested in the opening scene. As layers of representation entwine, Joey's statement reinforces both homophobia and racism; it appears that both O.J. and Joey have manipulated the system through unethical cries of injustice and both get away with murder—they can be said to have enacted a perversion of justice.

Even while gay sexuality was *central* to the characters in the shows that I studied, it became visible only in the abstract through talk and through linkages with other discourses (e.g., misogyny). In this sense, homosexuality never concretely became visible but rather haunted (cf., Gordon 1997) the shows—much like it haunted my interviews. This haunting is about more than queer people passing as straight (cf., Gamson 1998). It is about a profoundly constant presence that is always just out of view.[13] Even the request for "sexual orientation" on my interview form gave an implied presence to multiple sexualities that was strong enough to evoke homophobia.

Like *The Practice, Judging Amy* had one gay character in the 1999 fall season, although in a much more marginal role. At a scene set at a holiday party (aired November 23, 1999) Hillary, a literary agent for Justin Hopkins and Vincent Gray, introduces the two writers to each other. After a brief talk about car mechanics at the buffet, they settle on a love seat, resting their plates of food on their knees as they talk. The loveseat in this scene provides a meaningful context for the ensuing interaction. Vincent, who is engaged in a jovial conversation with Justin (that interweaves jokes about mechanics, car repairs, and writing), looks up to see Hillary watching them. In the ensuing sequence, the camera alternates with the dialog, taking the place of the listener—producing a subjective image (Casetti 1999) that enables the audience to see the unfolding action alternately through the eyes of each man.

Vincent: Why is your agent staring at us?
Justin: I guess she wants to see how her project is working out.
Vincent: What project is that?
Justin: You and me.

> [*Vincent pauses and raises his eyes.*]

Justin: You don't know, do you?
Vincent: Know what?
Justin: You and I are so supposed to be fixed up.
Vincent: We are?

This sequence draws on the irony of mistaken identities: Hillary had mistakenly believed that Vincent was gay, while Vincent mistakenly believes that Justin is straight. In previous episodes, Vincent who is single, has repeatedly rejected increasingly persistent romantic overtures from Hillary, who is smart, charming, and conventionally beautiful—thereby bringing his heterosexuality into question. Vincent's failure to accept Hilary's advances—his failure to fulfill a heterosexual fantasy—is such an anomaly within the heterosexual imaginary that the only way to explain it is through recourse to something outside of hegemonic order. He must be gay. By contrast, in this episode, Justin's demonstrations hegemonic gender (established, both through his demeanor and conversation about car mechanics) enables the presumption of heterosexuality.

Justin's brief appearance on *Judging Amy* presents the opportunity for the show to assert the heterosexuality of one of its main characters, Vincent Gray. Vincent's heterosexuality is asserted three times in this episode: in his conversation with Justin, in a conversation with Hillary, and again at home. While Vincent asserts his sexual identity in his personal and professional relationships, his mother does so for him at home—when Vincent brings Justin home with him to the family Thanksgiving dinner. The family is laughing boisterously, and still gathered around the dinner table dotted with empty wine bottles, when Vincent's sister Amy arrives with Bruce Van Axel:

Amy: Hi everybody. This is my court services officer, Bruce.
Mrs. Gray: Hello Bruce. Happy Thanksgiving. This is my son Peter. And this is my soon to be ex-son-in-law Michael and his daughter Lauren, who is also my Amy's daughter. Amy made this delicious dinner. And this is a very nice gay man who we just met. And this is my son Vincent who is not gay. He's a writer.

At the moment when it becomes possible to imagine Amy, an apparently white woman, and Bruce, an apparently black man, as a couple arriving at Amy's home for Thanksgiving dinner, Amy's introduction delimits their relationship. She does not introduce Bruce, as Bruce, but as her subordinate ("this is my court services officer") whose name is Bruce. Despite its invisibility, disciplinary power necessarily presupposes regulatory *practices*, mechanisms of discipline; this excerpt illustrates how these mechanisms can appear in local contexts as the practical actions of participants. Consider Mrs. Gray's introduction of the "very nice gay man" marks the stigma it dismisses (i.e., he's a very nice man, even though he is gay). This casual outing of Justin implies a level of social acceptance that is simultaneously limited, if not denied, by the very introduction.

Since Vincent and Justin are seated side by side, Mrs. Gray's introduction of Vincent ("who is not gay" but a "writer") quickly clarifies the nature of their relationship. Vincent's sexuality is never asserted as straight or heterosexual, which would render it a notable category on par with gay. Rather, Mrs. Gray's introduction, "And this is my son Vincent who is not gay," asserts heterosexuality as the unspoken (i.e., natural) category. Once Mrs. Gray establishes Vincent as "not gay" she then establishes what he *is*—"a writer." This very brief dialog *repeatedly* naturalizes heterosexuality. First notice that only Justin's sexuality is made relevant in a round of first introductions. Second, in this introduction, Justin's sexuality eclipses everything else about him (e.g., he is not introduced as a writer). Third, there is the assertion that Vincent is "not gay" (as opposed to explicitly saying he is straight or heterosexual). Fourth, the sentence construction creates a structural anticipation for an analogous description ("And this is my son Vincent who is not gay. He's _____"). This construction calls to mind an invocation of straight or heterosexual, which is then subverted—heterosexuality is conjured up but not named. This repetition of heterosexuality marks its inherent instability (cf., Butler 1990, 1993). The dense reiteration of heterosexuality within and across television shows is again leveraged through the repetition of the television shows themselves via reruns, DVDs series, and iPod downloads. Central, of course, is the issue that heterosexuality is repeated in a variety of ways but never named. The unmarked nature of heterosexuality naturalizes a hegemonic "center" —from which all distances are measured by marked categories. Discourse constitutes subjugated subjectivities through marking "difference" from an unspoken norm. Hence, in this marking, the disciplinary power of heterosexuality is manifested through, and extended by, the process of identifying as gay, lesbian, or bisexual. The constant repetition of gender, the need to "tell the difference," can be understood as a way of guarding against a "difference that might otherwise put the identity of one's own position in question" (Garber 1992, 130).

Yet disciplinary mechanisms cannot always be so clearly traced in local practice. For instance, both of the gay characters on primetime shows were apparently white, and race functioned as the unmarked background of the show. One could argue whiteness became the condition of articulation, through which homosexuality was made visible in primetime television.[14] Further, if lesbians on *Ellen* might be said to have cracked-opened the door to nonhegemonic sexualities on primetime TV, one could also say lesbians and bisexuals seem to have been left standing outside the door. That neither lesbians nor bisexuals appeared at all in these nine shows makes it important to recognize that oppression works "not only through acts of prohibition, but covertly, through the constitution of viable subjects and through the corollary constitution of a domain of unviable (un)subjects—abjects, we might call them—who are neither named nor prohibited..." (Butler 1991, 20). Disciplinary power then is evident not only through the subjects it produces (Foucault 1978) but also through the production of "abjects." Simply to name the production of abjects one must exceed the limits of standard sociological analysis, for here again, we are left with absence as a discursive effect that does not leave material evidence.

To the extent that sex and gender are understood as synonymous, and gender and heterosexuality are understood as a single expression of "nature" (i.e., all people must be either women or men and are presumed to be heterosexual by virtue of their being women and men) alternative genders and sexualities become visible only through some form of subversion. Hence the conditions of heterosexuality produce both the apparent presence of dimorphic gender and the terms under which homosexuality and bisexuality can be made visible (cf., Foucault 1978; Frye 1983; Butler 1990). However, because attributions only made visible those people who were *not* heterosexual, they served to maintain the invisibility and apparent naturalness of heterosexuality. Consequently disciplinary power of heterosexuality was manifested by and extended through the very people being dominated by its discourse. The fact that the television shows I studied depicted gay men, but not lesbians or bisexual women, demonstrates one more way that discursive practices regarding gender produce both an androcentric and heterocentric reality.

The processes through which gender is produced as self-evident must be invisible—a matter of commonsense—in order to be successful. The function of discourse is to actualize subjects recognition of themselves, *as a matter of commonsense.* In order to disrupt heteronormativity, it is necessary to rupture the apparent naturalness of heterosexuality by naming it. *To name heterosexuality is to deprive it of the appearance of being natural, or inevitable, by forcing the identification to become visible.* Through this process of identifying persons as heterosexual, the naturalized center from which "difference" can be measured is shattered. Naming heterosexuality does not take us outside the system of knowledge produced through sexual categorizations. Rather, such naming deprives heterosexuality of normative status by refusing the apparent naturalness of heterosexuality and places it on par with other sexualities within that system.

To disrupt the naturalness of heterosexuality is to also disrupt the processes that naturalize gendered divisions of labor, since gendered divisions of labor are tied to the heterosexual family (Engels 1978; Hennessy 2000). "Woman's position as subordinate other, as (sexual) property, and as exploited labor depends on a heterosexual matrix in which woman is taken to be man's opposite..." (Hennessy 2000, 25). Hence, to rupture the apparent naturalness of heterosexuality is also to disrupt historical relations of family, labor, and consumption. Discursive practices, in talk and representation, link gender and sexuality together in ways that produce regimes of knowledge/power that sustain both an androcentric and heterocentric reality.

On Being Human

In the previous sections, I explored the production and consequences of commonsense knowledge that produces gender as both apparently pervasive and natural. Yet an understanding of commonsense knowledge about gender is incomplete without an analysis of how commonsense knowledge in interviews and media constituted some groups of people as being *without* gender. In this section, I examine how, and to what effect, commonsense forces specific erasures of gender. Because commonsense reflexively establishes conceptions of normalcy and community, commonsense can be deployed to systematically exclude many groups of people from a larger community. Practices that constitute some groups of people as being without gender are central to cultural production of gender.

In dominant, cultural discourse, commonsense knowledge produced some groups of people as being without gender in two ways: by establishing race as both more important and as oppositional to gender and through the use of nongendered characterizations and slurs. The first of these arose in interviews and television shows, while the later arose in interviews and newspaper articles. In a society where gender appears to be relevant at potentially every moment, commonsense knowledge that constitutes some groups of people as being *without* gender holds particular analytical and political significance. I begin by examining how hegemonic commonsense established race as both more important than, and as oppositional to, gender.

The Naming That Is Not

Throughout the course of my interviews, white people talked—implicitly and explicitly—as though all people of color were *men*. Consider this excerpt, for instance, where Captain Ahab, an attorney with an established reputation for social justice work, responds to my question about his work:

> *Celine-Marie:* It occurs to me as we are talking that you [...] certainly have a reputation as a champion of the underdog, that you have a pretty sterling reputation in town as somebody who fights the good fight. And I wanted to ask you...how your identity as a white man comes into play with this.
>
> *Captain Ahab:* Sometimes I wonder whether it creates a barrier for me in dealing with gender cases, by FAR the majority of my cases are women and always have been.

Even though I asked about Captain Ahab's work *vis á vis* his identity "as a white man," he characterizes his work with respect to gender, but not with respect to race. He went on to talk at length about his experience as a man dealing with potentially intimate issues regarding women. He never mentioned race. Because whiteness is an unmarked or assumed category in the talk and representations of white people, Captain Ahab's response implies that the "gender cases" he refers to are those of white women. Captain Ahab implicitly conflates women and whiteness by speaking only to one-half of my question—that of gender.

The association of women and whiteness appeared more explicitly when Lue Lani and I were talking about the possibility of having a person of color as president of the United States. She remarked, "I think we'll definitely have a black person in the presidency. I want to see a woman in there first." Through this comment, Lue Lani establishes an apparent contradiction between being a woman and being black. This apparent contradiction between being a woman and being black does not articulate an absence of black women; rather, it articulates the social value of black women in a white, patriarchal society. Lue Lani expresses a contradiction in a white cultural imagination between the *qualities* associated with blackness and those associated with women (cf., Hull,

Scott, and Smith 1982; Lubiano 1992). Indeed, there is an almost routine polarization of "blackness" and "womeness" (Crenshaw 1992).

Representations of gender in television also relied upon, and reproduced, similar implicit knowledge regarding black women. Consider this exemplar from the legal drama *The Practice*. In the 1999 series, *The Practice* featured three apparently white women and one apparently black woman in roles as strong and effective lawyers. On the level of visual representation, Rebecca Washington, the only woman of color on the show, is highly visible. But on other material and symbolic levels of representation she was invisible (cf., Cook and Johnston 1988; Lubiano 1992, 1997a). For instance, on a professional level, cultural assimilation makes Rebecca visible; she argues cases in the courtroom and interacts with co-workers and defendants. Yet, the show remains *socially* segregated. While friendships among white women attorneys (as housemates and confidants) become the occasional focus of the show, the character of Rebecca Washington has no social existence at all. Rebecca is the only woman on the show never to have had a romantic relationship. Because black women have suffered from white stereotypes of hypersexuality (Aptheker 1982; Carby 1997; Collins 1993; Crenshaw 1992; Davis 1983), this may seem like an improvement to some, or perhaps simply the other end of an extreme. Yet what is important in this context is that representations of Rebecca's sexuality set her apart from white women on the show and the hegemonic discourse that articulates gender. In addition, Rebecca has no friends, no family, no personal interests, or history. In this sense, Rebecca exists as a *worker*, not as a woman.

The Practice consistently focused on the victimization of white women—both in legal cases of rape and murder and in plots in which the white women attorneys themselves were victimized in the 1999 season. By the end of the fall episode the three white women attorneys each had survived homicidal assaults and the firm's receptionist, a young white woman, had been video-taped in her own shower by her landlord and bitten on her breast by her dentist when under anesthesia. In each of these scenarios, men in the office rose to the occasion to protect the women. Rebecca Washington was the only woman never to be victimized—or protected.

What makes Rebecca less vulnerable than all other women on the show? Formerly the firm's receptionist, Rebecca has the least experience, and is the least assertive and least confident of the women attorneys. Yet, Rebecca was never shown in need of mentoring, advice, or protection from men. Rebecca's apparent invulnerability sets her apart from white women yet it does not come from some extraordinary ability; Rebecca was not more accomplished or capable than her white counterparts. Consequently, it is important to ask if Rebecca suffers from the sort of invisibility Lue Lani articulated—an apparent contradiction between being both black *and* a woman.

Commonsense knowledge that reproduces dominant culture secures cultural hierarchies of race and gender. The binary of woman/man depends upon a discourse that produces "woman" as the opposite of "man." Hence, in dominant U.S. culture, the central cultural meanings of "woman" are produced through discursive formations that link together femininity, vulnerability, weakness, and gentleness—qualities opposite those of masculinity. At the same time, white hegemonic discursive formations in U.S. culture produce the meanings of blackness as the opposite of whiteness. The convergence of hegemonic gender and race discourses produces black woman as a contradiction in terms (cf. Carby 1997; Hull Scott and Smith 1982; Lubiano 1992). The liberal racism inherent in talk and representations that produce "women" and "blacks" as a contradiction in terms is not based on an explicit *feeling* of anger or hatred but rather is based on a particular way of *seeing* the world (cf., Goldberg 1993; Memmi 2000; Patai 1991). Yet there is more than a simple contradiction at work here. Whiteness is the unarticulated condition through which womanhood is produced. Consider, for instance, how Lorraine Doe, from the Paiute Nation, talked in our interview about her experience in a predominantly white elementary school:

> I think—because we were Indian—we had more freedom than probably most kids, because they didn't know what to do with us anyway. So, they would let us do it [play with the boys' toys] cause we didn't know any better. Whereas other little girls would know better, because they had been taught, and brought up in society, in a certain way, and WE hadn't. Yknow, we were just little HEATHENS.

The unmarked background of whiteness is the condition through which the racist slur "heathen" becomes a disciplining force that set Lorraine outside the hegemonic construction of gender. If Lorraine internalizes the racism by reflecting that the Indian girls "didn't know better" than to play with boys' toys, she also turns the disciplinary force back on white society by claiming a place of greater freedom.

As a further illustration of how whiteness functions as the unarticulated condition of gender, consider how Lorraine later described her efforts to help younger Native Americans to launch a protest one Thanksgiving to educate others about representations of "unisex Indians" in holiday cards.

Lorraine:	You know, from all of the Snoopy Indians that were... out there, you know, to the little animals that were Indians, and, um, pointing out, you know, the, uh, the unisex Indian. You know, in a picture you have... a little female pilgrim, with a bonnet, and then you have the little male, with the tall black hat, but you have the Indian with just a headband. So there is no—there is no gender there.
Celine-Marie:	Mmm.
Lorraine:	You know, he's just...Indian. You know, especially with animals. You know, I—when you dress up animals, they're most likely, the Indian is never... a—a female Indian, or a—a Indian male, they're just 'Indian.'

In the dominant cultural imagination, commonsense renders conflation of Native Americans with animals *not only sensible, but unremarkable.* Even here, Lorraine protests, not the conflation of Native Americans with animals, but the lack of gender.[15] To exist without gender is to exist outside of culture, outside of the conditions of subjectivity. The presence of gender not only marks heterosexuality, it marks cultural citizenship. Certainly, the discursive construction of Native American women and men as genderless heathens was essential to U.S. policies and practices of genocide. Even as a friendlier heathen appears on holiday cards, cultural violence against Native Peoples continues as is evidenced in severe poverty, unemployment rates over 80 percent on many reservations, and continued denial of national sovereignty and treaty rights.

You Gotta Have Class

Although the demands of the English language make it difficult to write about people and elide gender, reporters, when writing about people who cannot afford housing, frequently do just this. For example, they refer to those who are living on the streets as "trolls" (Bailey 1984); "transients" (Brisbane 1985; Williams 1994); "homeless adults," (Kerr 1985a); "river-bottom dwellers" (Levine 1994); "street youths" (Staff 1995); "street people" (Dolan 1994); and, "the homeless" (Bates 1994; Herman 1982; McMillan 1990). Reporters write about: "Scores of the homeless" (Goodwin 1983); "the new homeless" (Kerr 1985b); "the homeless problem" (Levine 1994); and "The number of homeless" (Alvarez 1995).

Since 1982, the term "the homeless" has taken root in public imagination and entered common usage as an apparently neutral term (i.e., a descriptive shorthand for complex social and economic relations).[16] Yet "the homeless" is not *just* a descriptive short hand, it is particular kind of phrasing that sharply focuses two discursive practices through which otherness is created and maintained. In media and interviews, references to "the homeless" were consistently juxtaposed against references to "people." For example, a newspaper article quotes a woman remarking on the change in management at a shelter where she was living: "The people who were here before... treated us real nasty. These people who are in here now, they care. They don't treat us like we're homeless—they treat us like we're people" (Loeb 1995, B1, B6).

If to exist without gender is to exist *outside* the bounds of citizenship in a particular place and time, to be home-less is to belong nowhere. "Homelessness" does not so much draw attention to a lack of housing as it does a lack of social networks, a lack of belonging. In daily life, no one—even those who cannot afford housing—is truly homeless. Hence, it is especially noteworthy that being unable to afford housing is characterized as homelessness, rather than houselessness. If housing is a commodity that one can afford—or not—a *home* is anything but a commodity. A home is a community, not just a collection of individuals, as is a household. A home is not so much a physical space as it is a rhetorical space of community and belonging.

> The (person or) character is at home when he (sic) is at ease in the rhetoric of the people with whom he shares life. The sign of being at home is the ability to make oneself understood without too much difficulty, and to follow the reasoning of others, without any need for long explanations. The rhetorical country of a (person or) character end(s) where his interlocutors no longer understand the reasons he gives for his actions, the criticisms he makes, or the enthusiasm he displays. A disturbance of rhetorical communication marks the crossing of a frontier, which should of course be envisaged as a border zone, a marchland, rather than a clearly drawn line (Vincent Descombes cited in Morley 2000, 17).

If people are no longer "at home" when those around them fail to understand their feelings, behaviors, and motivations, then truly people who cannot afford housing are not "at home" in the United States. It is through this profound lack of empathy that people unable to afford housing become "homeless." "Home" is a place of sustenance (Nash 1993), a place where one is cared for and cared about. In this sense, homelessness is a profound cultural rejection. In newspaper articles, poor people's resistance to hegemonic discourse surfaced in a few places. For instance:

"I'm not homeless!" Jenkins said yesterday, waving an arm toward the expanse of green lawn and golden sunlight around him in the Foggy Bottom area. "This is my home." (Guillermoprieto 1984, C1, C7)

In this quote Jenkins makes visible what others would deny him and calls to question the political nature of a home through the power of disidentification. Jenkins, resists the interpolation of homelessness by pointing to the space that is his home. Disidentification requires an awareness that stands outside of the commonsense knowledge it contests. The reporter, by including this quote, reiterates Jenkin's disidentification and through this reiteration the reporter *also* must visibly insert Jenkins in the article as a *gendered* person—a man, with a name. To be denied things so fundamental to social organization as gender and a home is to be placed completely outside of humanness. However, the discursive organization of social identities is always partial and fragmented—and hence, always open to resistance and subversion (Butler 1997a, b; Foucault 1977; Hall 1991).

Matters of Difference

The generative power of language comes, in part, from the ability of a single characterization or representation to invoke multiple discourses. Race, gender, class, citizenship, and sexuality all are discursively linked. The power of gender comes through constitutive practices that not only produce people as "naturally" women and men, but which also produce heterosexuality, homophobia, xenophobia, racism, and class discrimination. Because sexuality, and gender are *relations* of power, they produce and reproduce other concordant relations of power: they become the conditions of articulation for each other. In this respect, sexuality, and gender are more than axes of power that *intersect* with race and class—*they all are dialogically productive accomplishments*. There is no generic woman, but rather multiplicities of women each produced, minimally, through discourses of gender, nation, race, sexuality, and class. The constitutive practices of gender are anchored through a multiplicity of sites and a repetition of strategies.

At the start of this chapter, I framed research on gender as falling into two broad epistemological frameworks: material feminism (i.e., social constructionist) and poststructural feminism. I drew this distinction (even though there are many significant differences within each framework) because they are separated by fundamental differences regarding the nature of subjects, and concordantly, the theorization of power and agency.[17] The materialist analysis secures agency by designating a preexisting (socially constructed) subject. The identity/subjectivity of women is historically constructed as an *a priori* fact and scholarship largely concerns the experiences of women and the inequalities attributable to gender.

The epistemological presumption of a foundational subject in material feminism has lead material feminists to criticize the poststructuralism's deconstruction of that subject as an effort to deprive marginalized people of a collective voice at the very moment when such groups have gained some measure of political power. However, doing away with foundational notions of the subject does not mean the end of collective voices. While commonsense leads us to believe that experience is a foundational category of social existence, it is "only through the way in which we represent and imagine ourselves that we come to know how we are constituted and who we are" (Hall 1993, 111). To say that subjects are constituted through discourse does not do away with social collectivities but deprives them of an *a priori* existence. Understanding how subjects are constituted forms the *precondition* of agency because to be constituted by language is to be produced within a network of power/discourse that is open to resignification. The subject is neither a ground nor a product but the permanent possibility of a resignifying process (Butler 1995, 47). To deny the ontological essentialism of identity is not to silence those who have begun to speak but to locate discourse as "the horizon of agency" (Butler 1995).

I want to argue here, as I have elsewhere, that a strategic multi-level analysis of commonsense knowledge, makes it possible to examine lived experience while critically analyzing the discourses through which experience is constituted. The quest for social justice in this framework begins by asking: If identity is always normative and therefore exclusionary, how do we conduct what Foucault called a "critical ontology of the self"? How does one take stock of the discourses through which subjectivities are produced, and then re-imagine oneself differently? Chapters 4 and 5 take up this challenge.

4

CLASS

A REPRESENTATIONAL ECONOMY

The gap between rich and poor in the United States has arguably exceeded the capacity to sustain meaningful democracy. Congressional Budget Office data show that, after adjusting for inflation, the average after-tax income of the top 1 percent of the population rose by $576,000 or 201 percent—between 1979 and 2000; the average income of the middle fifth of households rose $5,500, or 15 percent; and the average income of the bottom fifth rose $1,100, or 9 percent (Center on Budget and Policy Priorities 2003).[1] In daily life this disparity is embodied in the struggles of African American, Native American, Native Alaskan, and Hispanic families that, according to the U.S. Census Bureau, have *median* household incomes $10–20,000 below government-based calculations for self-sufficiency. The disparity is embodied in the struggles faced by 40 percent of poor single-parent working mothers who paid at least half of their income for child care in 2001(Center on Budget and Policy Priorities 2003); in the struggles of 4.9 million families who paid half of their income in rent in 2002 (National Alliance to End Homelessness 2002); and, in the struggles of more than 3.7 million adults with disabilities living on federal Supplemental Security Income (SSI), which now provides less than one-third the income needed for one-bedroom apartment (O'Hara and Cooper 2003, 11). Minimum-wage workers, in 2002, were unable to afford a one-bedroom apartment in any city in the nation. If the increase in poverty is apparent, the tremendous increase in wealth accruing to the top 1 percent of the population is extremely hard to track. While conditions of poverty may make the evening news, thorough reports on conditions of affluence are more unusual. The affluence and poverty that variously shape life in the United States are not part of a sustained or routine public discourse. In the United States, economic inequality—arguably one of the most *material* sites of "difference"—is often one of the least visible.[2]

If commonsense leads people to believe that we can recognize race and gender on sight, even if we might sometimes find ourselves confused or mistaken, commonsense about class operates quite differently. While people living in the extreme poverty of homeless make class visually recognizable, generally class is not apparent "just by looking" at a person, or in passing encounters. The presence of people who are homeless is arguably the most consistently clear display of class in daily life. If the observable presence of race and gender means that each can be made relevant at potentially any moment, the relative invisibility of class renders it far less likely to be made relevant.

By examining the cultural production of class, I do not mean to suggest that wealth and poverty have no materiality apart from language but rather, I argue that because material conditions and discursive practices are not ontologically distinct, understandings of class need to be rooted to language, as well as economics. To begin with, all objects and events are constituted as meaningful through language and representation (Butler 1997a, b, c; Hall 1997b, c, e; Laclau and Mouffe 1985; Volosinov 1973). An earthquake may be understood as a geological phenomenon or an act of god; a stone may be a marker, a sculpture, or geological evidence, depending on the meaning we give to it (Hall 1997c). Experience must be interpreted in order to become meaningful. The cultural discourses that enable people in the United States to make sense of wealth and poverty cannot be separated from the materiality of that production. For example, in my initial analysis of media and interviews, representations of, and talk about, class appeared to be so completely dislocated from economics as to lack *any* concrete mooring. Indeed, everyday assumptions about class appeared to be idiosyncratic. Scholars have often raised the specter of "false consciousness" to describe a lack of class-consciousness. Yet it is important to recall there was a time in U.S. history when cogent class analyses shaped public discourse (cf., Piven and Cloward 1979; Foner 1988, 1990, 1995). The disappearance of such public discourse cannot be separated from a class history shaped by the government's consistent willingness to use deadly violence against workers and unions through deployment of the National Guard and federal troops. Although we "forget" it, we begin talking about wealth and poverty within a preexisting discourse shaped by class struggle.

In this chapter, I analyze commonsense knowledge about class in order to understand that which people must assume in order to live in a country that is devoted to the rhetoric of democratic equality, yet divided by the disparities produced through an equal commitment to competitive prosperity. In order for class differences to be generally invisible, there must be a systematic detachment between the social displays and economic productions of class. I begin by focusing my analysis on basic questions: In what ways, and on what terms, does commonsense knowledge make class positions (our own and others) recognizable? How is it that people recognize, or fail to recognize, themselves and others as members of socio-economic classes? I examine how commonsense knowledge about class in the United States leads people to engage in practices that systematically disorganize the presence of social and economic capital. By analyzing commonsense understandings of class, I unsettle epistemological traditions of economic determinism and move toward more complex, fluid conceptualizations that incorporate discursive, representational aspects of class.

What Constitutes Class?

Sociological class theory remains anchored by three theorists: Marx, Weber, and Dahrendorf. Marx's intellectual efforts were directed toward understanding capitalism, the capitalist state, and the exploitation of workers (Marx 1978, 1990). Many contemporary Marxist scholars have attempted to improve Marx's work by accounting for the changing conception of the working class and the contingent controversies regarding the development, definition, function, and meaning of the middle class (Poulantzas 1975, 1982; Przeworski 1978, 1985; Wright 1989, 1997). Cox (1959) and Bonacich (1972) attempted to extend Marx's analysis to account for race by including analyses of racialized divisions among workers, while Gordon (1982) incorporated analyses of race and gender through theorization of primary and secondary job categories within companies that reproduce race and gender hierarchies.

By contrast, Weber (1978, 1995) developed a detailed description of social and economic stratification that advantaged owners of goods (wealth) rather than the owners of production, per se. Consumption, rather than production, is the causal element in Weber's theory of stratification. From yet another perspective, Dahrendorf (1959, 1967, 1979) developed a social and economic analysis based on the distribution of power and authority. More recently, feminist scholars have transformed class theory by including gendered analyses (Acker 1973; Davis 1983; Eisenstein 1990; Hartmann 1982) and by challenging Marxist notions of "productive" labor by using precapitalist analyses as a cornerstone for understanding the division of labor (Mies 1986; Mitchell 1990). While some feminist scholars argue that patriarchy and white supremacy are systems of oppression that interlock with capitalism (Collins 1993; Dill 1992; Glenn 1985), other feminist scholars contest the model of "interlocking oppressions" asserting that identity is not a three-part experience of multiple selves (race/class/gender), but a coherent whole whose reality is shaped by one's effort to make sense of experience (Bannerji 1995; Guillaumin 1995; Fenstermaker et al. 1991). In addition, scholars and activists from Indigenous Nations (Dirlik 1996; LaDuke 1995; Trask 1993) have argued that while the exploitation of Indigenous Peoples has been, and continues to be, central to capitalism, the concerns of Indigenous Peoples have not be addressed by theories of class, or by the intersectional paradigm of race/gender/class.[3]

Cultural critiques of class (cf., Bourdieu 1996) mark a significant turn from analyses of relations of production and exploitation to analyses of cultural capital. Yet historical conceptions of class, both as material and cultural capital, have been challenged further by new epistemological and ontological frameworks. For example, Watkins (1998) examines the commonsense practices through which people make sense of their economic worlds, and Fiske (1999) uses a semiotic framework to analyze homelessness. Taking a cultural studies approach to class, du Gay (1996) reimagines positions of "consumer" and "employee" to reconsider class of identity and subjectivity. Other scholars (cf., Bettie 2003; Gibson-Graham 1999; Pascale 2005) depart radically from classical analysis of class to variously explore class as performative. This chapter extends performative analyses of class.

You Don't Say: Theorizing Commonsense

In this section, I examine how middle-class identities are produced and naturalized in ways that are unrelated to economic circumstances. For instance, most people I interviewed characterized themselves as middle class—regardless of whether they were multimillionaires or blue-collar workers. While this might strike readers as itself a matter of commonsense, rather than as a point of analytic interest, it is possible to understand this information as something more than a cliché. Toward that end, let me begin by saying that four of the five multimillionaires I interviewed characterized themselves as middle class and asserted that perceptions of them as wealthy were mistaken. (I will come back to this exception later in the chapter.) For example, Brady, a white attorney specializing in estate planning explained: "I guess we define class by wealth since we don't have nobility here. So [...] I guess I'm in the middle, based on our tests, our society, probably middle class."[4] I found it difficult to think of Brady, with assets of nearly $5 million, as "in the middle" of the economic spectrum. As Brady continued, he described upper-class people as "pretentious" and added: "I don't feel class is that important and I don't care for folks who think it is." Brady's dismissal of class is not so much a denial of his wealth but a dismissal of the "folks" who make wealth the measure of a person. Similarly, Polard, a white commercial real estate developer, distinguished his wealth from his personality. He talked about himself as "middle class" and called himself "an average kinda joe" who "eats hamburgers at McDonalds." Polard did not just call himself "average" but invoked a discourse that links him to a certain kind of masculinity. Polard elaborated: "I don't feel a connection to I guess what one would consider upper class. I don't feel connected to that. You know, my friends—my relationships—and that, are middle America." Throughout the interview, Polard reinforced a distinction between the kind of person he is and the wealth that he has. For instance, Polard said:

> When uh you live in this house [...] the average person driving down the street will view the big house with all the land sitting on an expensive street, [and think] he must be very rich. But I mean that's not me, it isn't my personality. [...] I'm just an ordinary kinda guy.

Polard is not denying his wealth; on the exit interview form, he valued his assets at over $100 million. Yet Polard displaces economic considerations of class by centering personal values. From eating at McDonald's to his personal relationships, Polard lays claim to a *class* identity that stands apart, or is made to stand apart, from his wealth.

Polard and Brady talk about "being middle-class" as being *a particular kind of person*—rather than as being a particular level of income or assets. Certainly, the routine nature of daily life leads most people to think of themselves as average (Sacks 1992). While it would be quite easy to press the claim that Polard is deluding himself (or me) by characterizing himself as "middle class," such a claim would foreclose important questions. In particular, on what terms, or in what contexts, do people characterize themselves by a *class* category that is independent of their economic resources? How might such misrecognition of class (willful or not) create a cultural quarantine that prevents critical questions, and opposing interpretations, from arising, or being seriously engaged?

While the rhetoric that people invoke when talking about class may be race and/or gender specific (e.g., "an average joe"), I sought and examined patterns of commonsense about class that transcended boundaries of race and gender. So, it is important to note that white men were not the only multimillionaires to characterize themselves as middle class. Two women, one Latina and one American Indian, who were self-made multimillionaires expressed similar sentiments. Marisol Alegria owned two burger franchises at the time of our interview. Marisol explained:

> In the community here, um, I find that there's a lotta respect for that [owning and operating fast food franchises]. Sometimes it's a misconceived respect, I think, an' especially in my case, because the perception is, "Oh my gosh, there's a lady that must be a multimillionaire." Or, you know, "That lady's just making beaucoup bucks," you know, and—and that kind of a thing. But it really, um—and there ARE some out there. I mean, because most of my counterparts throughout, are REALLY in the big buck category.

Marisol talks about herself as the object of "misconcieved respect" based on a false perception. Yet, she is a self-made multimillionaire with assets worth just under $10 million. It seems possible that Marisol can argue that perceptions of her as wealthy are "misconceived" by comparing herself to even wealthier peers. Certainly, "beacoup bucks" and "big bucks" are relative terms that avoid any fixed notion of wealth. However, Marisol also resists being perceived by others as a multimillionaire—a very specific category and one that is consistent with her own characterization of her assets. It seems unlikely then that Marisol is invoking a purely relative notion of wealth, or that she is trying to conceal her wealth in the interview. Since Marisol objects to the *perception* that she is a multimillionaire, it seems possible that she does not believe that she is *recognizable* as a multimillionaire—that in social environments she does not stand out as different. It is not just that class, seen from within, can be imagined to be invisible but that *markers of class can be disorganized in such a way as to make class unintelligible.* Indeed, Marisol later talked about the care that she takes with her appearance so that she does not stand out.

Marisol: I have a wonderful, and I really feel very good about this, I have a wonderful experience at mixing very well. I could be with the richest of the rich and not drop the beat, not feel intimidated, or uncomfortable.
Celine-Marie: Mmhm.

Marisol: You know, I know that I have an outfit or two that would
wear just as well. And if were going to... uh, one of my
employee's baptismals, out in Las Viejas I know that I could
wear, you know, something there to not intimidate or feel...
you know, as though I'm out of... out of class there,
Celine-Marie: Mmhmm.
Marisol: or would intimidate the guests or anything else.
Celine-Marie: Mmhmm.
Marisol: I think I can do that very well. So... for that reason, I think
I...I just kinda... mesh very well.

Here one can better see why Marisol might object to the *perception*
that she is a multimillionaire. Marisol talks about herself as someone in
the middle. She can socialize with the "richest of the rich" and not "feel
intimidated" and can attend a social gathering hosted by one of her fast
food employees without intimidating the other guests. Marisol talks
about class as a social category based on interaction; to intimidate or be
intimidated is "to be out of class."

Lorraine Doe, an American Indian who worked as a tribal adminis-
trator, also talked about herself as being middle class based on being an
"average" person. At the time of our interview, she held assets of over
$500 million. It is not just that Marisol, Lorraine, Polard, and Brady
think of class in purely personal terms but that in order to maintain
their ordinariness, they *must* think of class in that way. And, in this
sense, their personal identity as ordinary people is in conflict with a
class location based on extraordinary wealth.

In order to produce and maintain the appearance of a class identity,
people must understand and manipulate complex meanings attached
to work, wealth, consumer goods, and other commodified cultural
forms. Recall, for instance, that Polard described himself as "an average
joe who eats hamburgers at McDonalds" and Brady referred to "folks"
rather than to "people." While theories of cultural capital (cf., Bourdieu
1996) help us to understand the manipulation of these symbols, discursive analysis illustrate the processes through which objects and
knowledge *become* cultural capital. Inflecting an analysis of commonsense knowledge about class with ethnomethodological and poststructural discourse analysis links together local practices and discursive
resources can provide insight into how class symbols, knowledge, and
identities are constituted as meaningful.

In all but one of the nine television shows that I studied, representations of daily life consistently divorced occupation and income
from assets, social resources, and opportunities. Here again, one must

exceed the limits of standard sociological "data analysis," in order to say anything about the dislocation of class and wealth. For instance, in *Judging Amy*, Judge Amy Gray's career success (as the youngest judge to be appointed to a family court bench) appears to have produced no more substantial material rewards than a Volvo station wagon. During the 1999 season, Judge Gray lived with her daughter and her mother, in her mother's house.[5] Similarly, on *The Practice*, the career success of lawyers and judges was not shown in relation to material wealth such as cars, houses, vacations, or hobbies. In the few episodes in which the audience enters an apartment that two women attorneys share, the shots are narrowly framed, making it difficult for the viewer to get any sense of the room beyond the bed, hallway, or bathtub. Work appears to be its own reward for attorneys at "one of the most successful criminal defense firms in Boston." Interestingly, when I asked people in my interviews what they liked about their work, consideration of material reward was equally absent. For central characters in legal dramas, their membership in a professional class provides a particular set of collegial relationships, but no distinctive economic benefit. As in interviews, socioeconomic class is represented through personalities, not through particular kinds of opportunities, activities, or possessions.

While the legal dramas I studied divorced professional careers from material rewards, comedies presented worlds in which any amount or kind of work could produce wealth. In *Ladies Man*, Jimmy runs a woodworking business in his garage that supports a family of four in a large and luxurious home with a swimming pool, and affords the family the ability to hire a private swimming instructor to provide lessons in their backyard pool. In *The Hughley's*, Milsap, whose line of work is not clear, begins the 1999 season living in a rented apartment and driving old pickup truck (aired October 1, 1999). He launches a romance with a wealthy woman, Regina, and when he gives her the key to his apartment this exchange ensues:

Regina: Oh this is so sweet and what a surprise.
Milsap: Well, I just figured it was about time.
Regina: No, I mean I'm actually surprised that you lock that stuff up.

Milsap's relatively poorer circumstances are established through this exchange, which occurs in the front seat of his old pickup truck. Later in the same episode, when Milsap decides he has to impress Regina to "keep her," he buys a 3,200-square-foot house with a tennis court in a wealthy neighborhood. Because the ability to make such a purchase is portrayed as if it were unrelated to work, savings, or income, it appears to be the sort of thing that anyone could do if they wanted. In the world of comedic fantasy, the only thing stopping Milsap from owning such a home in the past was his own desire.

In *Frasier,* comedic tensions produce class differences through competing productions of white masculinity. Historically, discourse about class generally has been discourse about white masculinity (cf., Acker 1973; Aptheker 1982, 1989; Davis 1983; Bannerji 1995; Guillaumin 1995; Pascale 2001). It is, therefore, not surprising that the clearest expression of class tension in the television shows I studied was among white men. The fact that this tension exists between a father and his sons reinforces the common notion of class *mobility* in the United States and mitigates the potential for more serious class conflict. Hence, the appearance of class difference is produced through relationships that also simultaneously limit or sanction conflict. Class conflicts between Martin and his sons do not concern economic inequality but rather personalities and preferences. For instance, in *Frasier,* when Frasier and his brother Niles protest their father's efforts to plan his own funeral, Martin responds:

> I realized that if I let you plan my funeral that it will be all harps, white wine, and frankly a lot of pissed off cops. [...] I got the whole service mapped out it will start with a bagpipe marching down the isle. And none of that dainty finger food either, big slabs of roast beef—prime rib. (Aired October 21, 1999.)

Martin doesn't advocate a less expensive or smaller funeral production but rather one that speaks to a different kind of man. Indeed, Martin seems to repeat the same discourse invoked by Brady and Polard. In *Frasier,* the class differences between father and sons are inseparable from productions of white masculinity. In both television and interviews, wealth appears to threaten a particular kind of masculinity.

Away from home, Frasier makes himself recognizable as "upper class" through overt displays of status. Consider an episode that opens in a hospital emergency room, where Frasier is waiting to be seen regarding an injury to his nose (aired November 18, 1999). He has spent his time in the waiting room comically trying to avoid a casual conversation with an apparently working-class man. After waiting some time to be seen by a doctor, he approaches the receiving desk and this exchange occurs:

> *Frasier:* Yes hello this is Doctor Frasier Crane here, I was just wondering, I filled out my paper work about half an hour ago....
> *Attendant:* They'll call you. They're seeing people in order of importance.

Frasier: Oh really, well you know, I DO have my own radio show.
Attendant: The importance of the INJURY.
Frasier: Oh yes, of course.

In this scene, Frasier's upper-class status is produced through overt sense of self-importance conveyed through his use of a title, and formal speech pattern. In addition, his clothing, in particular his suit and overcoat that appear to be both more expensive and more formal than clothes others are wearing, sets him apart from all other people in this scene. Frasier's exaggerated display of self-importance and professional success is immediately sanctioned. The scene derives its humor both from Frasier's pomposity and the quick sanction it evokes. *Frasier,* the only show to make material wealth the central theme in its narrative and comic structure, consistently draws its humor from sanctions against overt displays of wealth/status and from contrasts between working-class and upper-class versions of white masculinity. Consequently, in *Frasier,* the discursive practices that make wealth visible also invoke its own censorship.

Although one segment of *60 Minutes* (aired October 17, 1999) concerned potential regulation of the pharmaceutical industry and framed this legislative effort in terms of the needs of poor senior citizens, by and large, the news magazines I studied (*60 Minutes, 60 Minutes II,* and *20/20*), either omitted, and hence rendered discussions of wealth and poverty irrelevant to news stories, or employed practices that reduced class difference to matters of personality. One *60 Minutes* (aired October 31, 1999) segment on a genetically transmitted disease, Retinitus Pigmentosis (RP) that causes progressive blindness in adults provides an excellent example of how wealth and poverty appear as a matter of personality. In this segment, Morley Safer interviewed three apparently white men, each of whom have RP. The segment begins with the camera on Morley Safer, who says:

> Tonight we take at look at some people who are taking a look at blindness. Three men. Three more different men you cannot find. Jim, a downtown, New York character.
> [*A voice-over continues as the camera cuts to Jim sitting alone in a bar. He is smoking a cigarette and sitting in front of a nearly empty glass of beer; daylight shines through the windows.*]
> The fringes of life is where he feels at home and what he writes about. [*pause*] Gordon as uptown as you can get.
> [*Voice over continues and camera shows Gordon attending a basketball game and interacting with Cavelier players. Safer's voice cuts out,*

*and we are given the sounds of game and a broadcaster shouting as a
Cavalier "hooks it up and scores!" Safer's voice cuts in again.*]
Millionaire businessman, eastern establishment, chairman of the
NBA, owner of the Cleveland Cavaliers. [*pause*] Issac, son of Cuban
immigrants,
[*Voice over continues and camera cuts to Isaac, head down and writing in a room full of books.*]
super achiever, Harvard Law. Destined for greatness. So different and
yet they share the common bond of a terrifying genetic accident and
each of them copes with it in his own particular way.

This opening segment does not introduce RP (Safer does not mention it); rather it introduces "difference" ("Three more different men
you cannot find"). While these men all have RP, Jim depends on dis-
ability payments, Gordon is a multimillionaire, and Issac is "a poster
child for the American Dream." Given this introduction, it would seem
logical to believe that the newsworthy "difference" among these three
men would be related to class. But this is not the case. Instead, Safer's report personalizes the substantive differences between them. For
instance, Safer introduces Jim—alone in a bar, drinking beer during the
day—as "a character." Only much later does the audience learn that Jim
is a writer who continues to write and to publish, despite his extremely
limited resources for accommodating his blindness. By contrast, Safer
introduces Gordon, a "[m]illionaire businessman, eastern establishment, chairman of the NBA, owner of the Cleveland Cavaliers" during
the excitement of basketball game in which the team Gordon owns is
winning. Safer introduces Issac, the "super achiever" who is "destined
for greatness" apparently hard at work and surrounded by books. The
meaning of the differences among these men is told through the story
of progressive blindness.

The show presents Gordon as a winner: confident, intelligent, and
good humored. Safer's affection for Gordon is evident in his enthusiasm
for, and curiosity about, his life; Safer expresses amazement at Gordon's
ability to recognize a member of his basketball team in conversation.
The audience sees Gordon enjoying breakfast in a large, sunlit area as
someone reads the *New York Times* to him. We see clips of him interact-
ing with family, skiing down a snowy slope, fly fishing in a river, and
conferring with medical researchers whom he is funding to find a cure
for RP. Safer acknowledges that, for Gordon, wealth provides "access to
assistance few others can afford" but, Safer says, wealth "was of no use in
stopping the blindness." By framing wealth in such a limited way, Safer is
able to place Gordon on equal footing with the other men in the story—
as if all three men faced the same fate. Gordon's economic privilege is

wiped away at the moment when the meaning of class difference comes to light. Gordon's confidence and cheer as he copes with progressive blindness can now be read as evidence of the kind of person he is—part of his personality, unrelated to the benefits of his economic resources.

The news segment then turns to Issac, who still has his sight, and Safer says: "The Lidsky family, Betty and Carlos and their four children are a kind of poster family for the American Dream." Issac's life comes together in a montage of clips: a successful career as a child actor, Harvard Law School at twenty years of age, close relationships with his parents and siblings, his discussions with medical researchers, and his public testimony before Congress. Isaac expresses undiluted optimism for his future and gratitude for his family. His hopefulness appears to be part of who he is, a part of who he would be, regardless of his life experience.

Safer then segues to Jim, the poorest man in this trio by saying: "If Isaac Lindsky looks to the sunny side of the street, Jim Knipfel seeks out the potholes." The camera follows Jim from a bar to his dingy, one-room apartment, lined with books. Safer continues: "He is a self-professed grump with a lot to be grumpy about. At thirty-three, he's spent his life fighting depression, alcoholism, and RP." Unlike the "super-achieving" Issac, Jim is legally blind and unable to read the books that surround him. He is the only interviewee who does not appear with family members; he has no special access to Congress, or to medical researchers. And, Jim is the only person to require public assistance both for medical care and daily living needs. But *60 Minutes* does not pursue the effects of these differences. Rather, the segment is concerned with the differences in the men's *attitudes* toward RP—differences that are represented as reflections of who they are. In this sense, the advantages and disadvantages of economics were personalized as matters of attitude (cf., West and Fenstermaker 1995a).

Television brings us, as viewers, into a quasi-fictional place—a virtual reality in which a woodworker's garage-based business can provide greater financial rewards than a career as a lawyer or a judge. In this virtual reality, the discursive production of class severs linkages between occupation, education, opportunity, and wealth to create class as a personal matter of character and will. Local practices draw on discursive resources to constitute a middle class filled with average or typical people—regardless of their wealth or occupation. To the extent that to be average in the United States is to be white, whiteness functions as the condition of articulation for representations of the middle class. That is to say, middle-classness is raced white through the forms of family, leisure, and consumption that make it visible.

Outside the Middle Class

Among the five multimillionaires I interviewed, Charlie Chin, a land and business developer, stood as the exception. Charlie identified himself as a first-generation Chinese American and talked about himself as anything *but* ordinary. Charlie, with assets over $10 million, was the only multimillionaire to categorize himself as "around the top" in terms of class. He described himself as a person who enjoys socializing among university presidents, hospital administrators, and government officials. Whereas other multimillionaires articulated a gap between the way others might perceive them based on wealth, and the kind of person they *really* are, Charlie made no such distinction. Charlie was also the only multimillionaire to talk about wealth as a means to overcome the vulnerabilities racism, immigration, and poverty. For instance, Charlie explained:

> I think that if you were a Mexican or Chinese immigrant and you don't have a great command of the language or let's say you have a command of the language but you slip up a little bit with your words or your tenses, things like that and you go to a hospital…you're treated differently than if I go in there. […]
>
> So I'll go into the hospital and I'll KNOW the doctor. Ok? Or, I'll know the other doctors there. I'll know the HEAD of the HOSPITAL. Ok? […] Whereas if you go in and you look like you don't belong or you can't pay your bill or um or you're not going to cause them a problem if they leave an instrument in your stomach or something like that…it's just, it's just COMPLETELY different. […] I think you will live longer. […] I think you will be cheated less, you will be treated with more respect, you will get faster service, and they will make sure that YOU don't die. […] That's why I work hard so I can take care of myself and my family and my extended family [big inhale] in that, in that manner. Also I KNOW that that's rotten and so I like to do things so that everybody gets a certain type of respect and care and consideration, too. Because what kind of society do you live in if it's too, too far that way?

Charlie Chin's strong identification with the experiences of immigrants, racism, and poverty produces *disidentification* with hegemonic class discourse, even as he celebrates the benefits of wealth. Indeed, it is the work of disidentification that makes his class privilege visible. Charlie Chin's celebratory success emerges from a history of legal exclusions in the United States that once prevented his parents, aunts, and uncles from the rights of citizenship, property ownership, and fair employment. In addition, Charlie's family was consistently vulnerable to the physical, emotional, and economic violence of racists. While, one might say Charlie Chin is a poster child for the American Dream, in his talk about class, he does not identify with the notions of equality and fairness that permeate the mythology of the American Dream. Nor does he identify with the mythic middle class. Rather, Charlie effectively resists hegemonic class discourses and resituates the competitive prosperity of the American Dream within historical processes of racism and economic oppression. This particular practice of disidentification is possible because class identification is constituted within various, often competing, systems of representation that carry forward different parts of histories.

Excepting Charlie Chin, people who did not identify themselves as middle class resisted characterizing themselves by class at all—regardless of whether they eventually categorized themselves as above or below the middle. For example, Lana Jacobs, a highly successful artist who held assets of nearly $1 million at the time of our interview, illustrates this point. Lana continued to make her home and studio in the working-class community of color, where she had lived before her success as an artist. While, she freely characterized herself as an artist, as black, and as a woman, Lana refused to characterize herself by class. Lana explained:

> I guess I am a universal person. I don't see myself fitting into a group. I am not a group-minded kind of person. [...] I feel stifled by groups because I have my own...my own attitude about uh what I feel what I know I lived. [...] I try not to judge. I work on my judgments about people.

Lana talked about class as a voluntary social category—something she could refuse to join. If Lana experiences being a woman, an artist, or black as a social *fact,* she talks about class as a social *judgment.* However, the unwillingness of the people I interviewed to characterize themselves as wealthy or poor should not be confused with their willingness to characterize others as such. Lana had no difficulty characterizing her grandparents as "a little below middle class." Yet being *a little* above or below the middle is an assessment comparatively free of judgment since to be in the middle is to be like most other people. By contrast, if Lana were to characterize herself by assets and wealth, she would be far more than "a little above" her family and community. By resisting class categorization, Lana implicitly asserts her long-standing connections to family, neighbors, and friends.

Similarly, when I asked Cuauhtemoc, a part-time stock clerk, if he had a class identity, he explained:

I consider myself a full-blooded Mexican but as far as a class...money's not a big thing to me, yeah we need it and everything but you know if it wasn't around or whatever, things would be a lot better. You know uhm...I think, I don't really consider myself a class, I think I'm more, I think I'm really ...how would you say it, privilege who I am and what I have you know, because no, I don't have a lot of money but I have what I need.

Cuauhtemoc advances his identity as "full-blooded Mexican," yet, like Lana, dismisses the importance of class identification. Interestingly he explains that he "privileges" who he is and what he has *because* he doesn't have a lot of money. If "not having a lot of money" conjures images of need or poverty, Cuauhtemoc also quickly dispels those images by saying "I have what I need." The class identifications most readily available to him through U.S. hegemonic discourse would be poor or lower class—identifications more likely to diminish, than enhance, a sense of self.

All of the people I interviewed who experienced daily economic hardship resisted hegemonic class categories, sometimes by inventing new categories. Emerson Piscopo, was unemployed at the time of our interview. He offered a surprising response to my question about class.

Celine-Marie: Uh-huh. Do you have a class identity?
Emerson: Uh, meaning where, where I fit in to society?
Celine-Marie: Mhmm
Emerson: Um, I guess fore...forefront, I'm a transsexual,
Celine-Marie: Mhmm
Emerson: Transgender, transgender um, I'm since I'm still, I'm it just using hormones right now, and I have had surgery though, a hysterectomy, I guess I'm PART of the way there.

Initially, I was flummoxed by his answer. Had he misunderstood the question? Was he subverting a question he didn't want to answer? Was he refocusing the conversation to a topic more important to him? I came back to the issue later in the interview and reintroduced a question about his class identity. Emerson explained his family's economic circumstances this way:

I'm starting out, I just, I had that major surgery so I'm not backed by a year's worth of work and it affected us [short pause] financially greatly, and we are both trying to catch up. We're, we're doin' it, but we're struggling, basically. We're in the struggling class. Not, not POOR but somewhere in between poor and okay.

Emerson introduces his family's economic difficulties through news of his surgery and his loss of work; he offers an *explanation* even before mentioning the economic hardship. Emerson talks about "trying to catch up"—indicating that ordinarily, his family had more resources and then frames their efforts to "catch up" as successful, if incomplete. In this way, Emerson is able to describe economic hardship while resisting identification with poverty. He underscores this resistance by saying "Not POOR but somewhere in between poor and okay." Thus Emerson not only defines the conceptual space between being poor and okay as one of personal struggle, he constitutes the meaning of his experience in a broader economic and social context.

If Emerson's response appears to be an anomaly, or a strategy that might be adopted only by people in economic transition, consider this exchange with Captain Ahab, a senior partner in a successful law firm:

> *Celine-Marie:* Uh-huh. Where would you place yourself in terms of class?
>
> *Captain Ahab:* I am first of all an immigrant. I moved to the United States at age six from Canada but um moved from Canada to Florida so it was a fairly long move. And so I arrived in Florida, again you know as an immigrant, and with an accent and so went through that type of displacement. Was exposed to discrimination issues at that age. I can remember very clearly driving through the southern United States and having my parents explain to me uh about the situation involving segregation in the South. This would have been in 1952. [...]
>
> *Celine-Marie:* That's interesting. Where do you put yourself today in terms of class?
>
> *Ahab:* Uh...upper-middle class.

Captain Ahab, like Emerson, responded to my question in a way that deferred or deflected a discussion of class. Both men also displaced my question about class identity by responding with features of their identity that each felt to be more central than class: Ahab as an immigrant and Emerson as a transsexual. If class is important to either man, they seem anxious to privilege a representation of self that is not class-based.

When I pursued the conversation about class, Captain Ahab described his class identity this way:

> My wife is superintendent and principal of a school district, a one-school school district. She has a master's degree. I have a BA, an MA and

a JD. And probably we're more upper-middle class by education, than by finances. Uh but uh still I think in the overall scale, we'd probably be considered upper-middle class.

Ahab underscores education as the determining factor in his assessment of class and then seems to capitulate to an unwanted characterization as upper-middle class. While one might argue that hegemonic notions of class can be produced through education, in Captain Ahab's talk about class, educational attainments are made to eclipse economic ones.

Overall, the people I interviewed understood class as a social judgment, not just an evaluation of economic resources, but of their self. When talking about their own *class* identities, everyone (except Charlie Chin) used discursive practices invoking social criteria that masked, distorted, or rendered invisible, their economic circumstances—even though they each volunteered their income and assets on the interview form. Class—construed in very personal terms, as something social— depends upon corresponding discourses of free will, personal values, and individual choices. In asserting the *primary importance* of a "me" that stands apart from one's economic conditions, talk about class systematically hid from view the cultural, social, and economic conditions that structure access to jobs, income, and wealth.

Transforming Public Discourse: The Rise of Homelessness[6]

While television shows produced cultural fantasies of wealth, newspapers subdued cultural nightmares of poverty as they reported on homelessness. Although all interviewees and media all referred to "the homeless" when talking about people who cannot afford housing, in this section I focus on newspaper articles. Because public discourse on homelessness is relatively new, newspaper articles about homelessness offer an important opportunity to examine how discursive practices develop.[7] People unable to afford housing have not always been "homeless." For instance, through the 1970s, reporters used terms such as "drifter," "transient," "vagrant," and "bum" to refer to people who could not afford housing (Blau 1992, Campbell and Reeves 1999). New discursive practices accompanied the increased visibility and vast numbers of people living on sidewalks and in parks. In the 1980s, the words "homelessness" and "the homeless" entered common usage as descriptive shorthand for the complex social and economic relations that were emerging. By 1982, the concept of "homelessness" had begun to take root in public imagination, yet discursive practices in news articles continued to go through systematic changes over the ensuing decade. These changes did not occur in rigid lines—as if produced by an edict—but rather are characterized by periods of overlap with soft edges, as is generally the case with social transformations produced by broader, and less direct, hegemonic forces.

During the early 1980s, newspaper articles distinguished between the "old poor" (drifters, transients, vagrants, and bums), accustomed to life on the streets, and the increasing numbers of "new poor" who were victims of recent economic changes. Newspaper articles consistently characterized the "new poor"—"the homeless"—as a better "class" of poor person than their predecessors. For instance, papers commonly reported that the "new poor" had lost their jobs in a recent series of layoffs (Herman 1982, McCarthy 1982). The *Washington Post* carried an ironic headline announcing evictions of "middle-class" families and reported:

> One housing specialist, Scott Riley of the Council on Governments, estimates there are 33,000 households in and around Washington waiting for public housing or government rent assistance, a record number.
>
> There are public and church-run shelters, but they are few in number and many of the new poor cannot bring themselves to use them. Many suburban areas have no shelters anyway, and homeless people in Prince George's County, for example, are given bus or taxi fare into Washington to seek emergency housing. (Engel 1983, A6)

In this article, the refusal of the "new poor" to use public and church-run shelters is not framed as a refusal of shelter services; rather, readers learn that the "new poor cannot bring themselves to use" existing shelters that, presumably, "the old poor" are using. The article goes on to detail how "the new poor" are different from poor people of the past, and uses an embedded quote from a Prince George County deputy to make the point. "... the most common response he hears, he says is 'I was laid off from my job. These are working people not the normal people we usually have.'" Initially "the homeless" referred to people— unlike transients, drifters, and bums— who had lost their jobs and consequently their homes.

Single (white) men were reported to comprise 85 percent of the estimated 1.2 million people without housing in 1983 and were referred to as "economic refugees who have found it impossible to get work or affordable housing" (Peterson 1983, A16L). Overall, newspapers used "homelessness" as a term to characterize hard-working people who lost their homes because of structural economic changes and were deserving of some new level of attention. The *New York Times* quoted then-New York Governor Mario Cuomo as saying that he was committed to "giving the homeless the safe, clean shelter that is *a basic human right*" (emphasis added, Rule 1983, 11N).

During this period, reporting practices made specific individuals and families, who had recently become homeless, visible to readers. For instance, a new plan to assist indigent families was told through the experience of Mrs. Culley and her children (Norman 1983); the effects of welfare cuts for people without housing was animated by the personal stories of Mr. Richards and Mr. Czukoski (Robbins 1983); and teen homelessness was explained through the personal stories of Winky Walker and her friends (Belcher 1983). Through stories like these, newspapers introduced the nation to the daily experiences of ordinary people who were unable to afford housing. These practices were short-lived.

By late 1983, articles also began to attribute homelessness to non-economic causes. For instance, in November of 1983, the *New York Times* reported that government officials agreed that one-third of the people living on the streets were jobless, one-third suffered from chronic alcoholism, and one-third suffered from mental illness (Sullivan 1983). This new configuration of homelessness was accompanied by a reconfiguration of what counted as credible, journalistic evidence. Where economic explanations of homelessness had been tied to unemployment figures and housing costs, claims about substance abuse and choice were framed in terms of personal observations, generally made by high-profile officials. For example, the *Los Angeles Times* quoted Police Chief Daryl Gates as saying, "I think you have a lot of people out there who wouldn't use it [temporary housing] if it were available. I think they are really happy just plopping on our soil" (Overend 1983, 1, 2). Similarly, the *Washington Post* quoted President Reagan explaining that "One problem that we've had, even in the best of times, [...] is the people who are sleeping on the grates, the homeless who are homeless, you might say, by choice" (Williams 1984, A1, A4). The explanation of homelessness as the consequence of personal problems and choices, offered initially by public officials, proved to be a compelling piece of the emerging discourse on visible poverty. This historical revisionism transformed the homelessness of hundreds of thousands of people (by some accounts millions of people) from a recent and acute problem into a less troubling, chronic problem—a problem that was present even in "the best of times." Such an historical revision was essential to securing the characterization of homelessness as a "choice," and to the concept of "free choice" becoming a central component in discourse about homelessness.

Characterizations of homelessness as a willful act ruptured the tentative emergence of earlier discursive practices that linked visible poverty to structural, economic troubles. The apparent willfulness and irrationality of choosing homelessness strengthened burgeoning discursive links between poverty, mental illness, and substance abuse and effectively subverted the association of homelessness with structural, economic changes. If readers initially felt compassion for people being displaced from their homes and jobs, newspapers quickly raised the possibility that this compassion was misplaced, as articles framed homelessness as the result of willful laziness, drug abuse, and mental illness, rather than as the result of high rent, a loss of section-eight housing, low wages, unemployment, and underemployment.

Despite newspapers' sustained practice of clearly identifying statistics, research reports, and surveys when attributing homelessness to economic causes, newspapers continued to attribute homelessness to mental illness, personal choice, and substance abuse on the basis of unverified claims made by high-profile officials. Soon, articles simply stated that homelessness was as much a product of personal problems as it was a product of structural, economic problems (cf., Guillermoprieto 1984, Miles 1984).

As newspapers commonly attributed homelessness to substance abuse (Guillermoprieto 1984, Henry 1984), free choice (Williams 1984, Brisbane 1985), and mental illness (Purnick 1985, Rimer 1985), "the homeless" came to be shorthand for *all* people unable to afford housing. Distinctions between "the new poor," as suffering from structural changes, and the "old poor" (as drifters, transients, and bums) quickly collapsed and articles about structural causes of such poverty faded from view. The cultural meanings of visible poverty temporarily stabilized as the consequence of personal failings. Homelessness, framed as a range of personal frailties and failures, became a *social* problem, rather than an economic one—especially as people brought private behaviors (such as grooming and sleeping) into public realms.

Articles linking severe poverty to structural, economic problems reappeared as the nation continued to experience periods of economic downturn and further increases in the numbers of people unable to afford housing. Reporters, however, wrote about "the *new* homeless" (emphasis added, Kerr 1985a, May 1986) as a way to distinguish between people suffering from current economic troubles and those already unable to afford housing (i.e., "the homeless"). However, the accounts of "new" homelessness, produced by the latest economic downturn, also strengthened the revisionist history of contemporary poverty. For example the *New York Times* reported:

> The homeless are no longer the lone drifters and former mental patients who were the vast preponderance of that population just a few years

ago. In dozens of cities, including New York, Washington D.C., and Los Angeles, and even in rural communities, emergency programs for the homeless are being flooded by functioning adults and families with children (Kerr 1986, E5).

Consistently, articles characterized "the new homeless" as "functioning adults," "families," and "children"—in other words, the poor who deserve assistance (cf., Pascale 1995, Pascale and West 1997). While newspapers explained the poverty of the "new homeless" in relation to low wages (Stein 1986) and housing shortages (Ifill 1990, Rich 1990, Stein 1986), newspapers now described "the homeless" as the "lone drifters" and "former mental patients" they had once been juxtaposed against.

However, shortly after "the new homeless" had emerged in public discourse, they became relegated to the ranks of "the old poor"—people held personally responsible for their poverty. Newspapers once again ran articles quoting prominent, public officials impugning the character of people who could not afford housing. For instance, the *Washington Post* quoted then-Boston Mayor Raymond Flynn saying, "'Homeless shelters and city streets have become the de facto mental institutions of the 1980s and 1990s'" (Broder 1991, A2).

By the mid-1990s, homelessness was firmly linked to substance abuse, mental illness, and free choice—rather than to structural problems of wages, layoffs, and housing. Discourse on "the homeless" focused on unwelcome behavior, including ranting, urinating in public, bathing in fountains, stealing, and panhandling (cf., Williams 1994). Articles about homelessness during this period focused almost exclusively on the problems that homelessness posed for people with housing. The problem of homelessness became one to be addressed through social control, particularly in the form of laws regulating camping and panhandling (cf., Pascale 1995, Pascale and West 1997). Articles about the "new homeless" ended—at least temporarily.

Discursive practices about homelessness in newspapers produced and maintained poverty as a social problem related to particular kinds of *people* rather than as an economic problem related to affordable housing, employment, and a living wage. Particularly significant is that newspaper coverage stabilized an understanding of systemic poverty as the consequence of personal problems through a series of discursive changes. These changes, however, were not random adaptations, but the regularization of capitalist discourse on poverty. Newspaper articles only characterized "new" poverty as the result of systemic economic problems—and by definition, "new" poverty is destined to be short-lived. If the "new poor" are victims of the economy, the "old poor" are held personally responsible for failing to get out of poverty. To the extent that poverty is evidence of personal frailties and failures, the public *visibility* of people living in poverty is one more expression of failure—the failure to hide one's poverty.

It is important to note that the development of public discourse about homelessness did not merely distinguish between the circumstances that might drive people into poverty and "the kinds of people" who would remain in poverty. Discursive practices *stabilized* the meaning of systemic poverty as personal failure by briefly acknowledging and subsequently *erasing* the visibility of structural, economic causes. In this sense, what might appear to be competing discourses about the causes of homelessness—mental illness, poverty, and choice—functioned as essential components for normalizing the presence of people who cannot afford housing. Homelessness is produced through a particular social discourse that links capitalism and morality.

Commonsense knowledge about capitalism, and its attendant responsibilities, privileges, and moral obligations *precedes* and shapes talk about, and representations of, people who are unable to afford housing. The meaning of any situation—including the possibility of its being interpreted *as* a problem—is discursively determined by the array of pre-existing, possible solutions.[8] Morality, then, is a means, not to justify solutions, but to constitute *problems* for which solutions appear obvious. For example, news articles never suggested that socialism would be a solution to pervasive poverty. The discursive production of homelessness is a politicized vision of poverty that produces particular problems, deliberations, and interventions. Because discursive practices construct substance abuse, mental illness, and a lack of character as the *causes* of homelessness, they preclude, or evade, discussion of mental illness, substance abuse, and character "weakness" as the *effects* of homelessness.

While people chose to subvert identifications with poverty in interviews, in newspaper articles, a person's status as homeless preceded all other information about them—most generally, even their name. People without housing are commonly identified simply as: "the homeless" (Toth 1991, Bates 1994, Herman 1982, McMillan 1990). In addition, articles referred to a "homeless man" (Krikorian 1996), "homeless adults" (Kerr 1985b), and to "homeless people" (Barbanel 1987, Dolan 1994). By contrast, newspaper articles did not characterize other persons by wealth or by the status of their housing. These practices not only constitute wealth as the unmarked or assumed category, they also divide people into two groups: "the homeless" and everyone else. The national discourse about people who cannot afford housing is not so much one of wealth and poverty as it is one of community and alienation. It is in this sense that bigotry emerges as being rooted to a particular way of *seeing* the world, rather than to explicit feelings of anger or hatred about poor people.

The disciplinary regulation of class is produced, in part, through gender discourse as discussed in Chapter 3. To be a person is to be either a woman or a man—gender appears to be self-evident as "simply the nature" of persons (Pascale 2001).[9] The self-evident nature of gender appears in newspaper articles, where the use of personal pronouns quickly, and without problem or doubt, classifies individuals—even when other details do not. Only when people do not have housing, do reporters write about them as if they were neither women nor men. While the demands of the English language make it difficult to write about people and elide gender, newspaper articles about people who cannot afford housing frequently do just this. For example, they refer to those who are living on the streets as "trolls" (Bailey 1984); "transients" (Brisbane 1985, Williams 1994); "homeless adults," (Kerr 1985b); "river-bottom dwellers" (Levine 1994); "street youths" (Staff 1995); and, "the homeless" (McMillan 1990, Bates 1994, Herman 1982). Reporters write about: "Scores of the homeless" (Goodwin 1983); "the new homeless" (Kerr 1985); "the homeless problem" (Levine 1994); and "The number of homeless" (Alvarez 1995).

Disciplinary, or regulatory, practices not only produce poverty as a marked category, they also produce it as so inherently meaningful that it overshadows all else about a person—even something as basic as gender. In this sense, it is possible to understand "the homeless" as being on par with racial slurs used to dehumanize groups of people. While one might argue that the severe poverty of homelessness is a "master category" that overrides gender, it is important to notice that some poverty is clearly racialized and gendered. For instance, if "the homeless" is shorthand for a kind of poverty that eclipses gender, "the welfare queen" is a slur that centers both gender and race. "The homeless" is a characterization that is not racialized or gendered—and it is this unmarked status both in terms of race and gender—that calls forth the subject position of white men. To the extent that both whiteness and maleness are assumed or unmarked categories, "the homeless" can be understood as a reference to a population largely composed of white men. The characterization "the homeless" masks the people it makes visible—single, white men. In this sense, discourse about homelessness must be understood through a tension that connects the inability to afford basic housing, with the position of extraordinary privilege accorded to white men in dominant American culture. This tension is expressed in newspaper articles through discursive practices that cycle through both compassion for, and fear of, "the homeless." At best, the result is a national ambivalence that naturalizes the devastations of capitalism.

Although "the homeless" initially referred to a "better class" of poor person, someone who had a home and lost it, the meaning of homelessness was reconfigured in the 1980s through discursive links to substance abuse, mental illness, and free choice. Homelessness no longer conveys a sense of a home lost but rather a lack of place, a lack of home or community to which to return. In this respect, "the homeless" are fundamentally different from the "lone drifters" and "transients" who seem to be passing through, who seem to have wandered from a place where they once belonged. While people often leave home, to be *without* a home is to be universally alienated. For "the homeless" there is no historical sense of place, no home, no community to which to return.

In Chapter 3 I argued that "homelessness" does not so much draw attention to a lack of housing as it does a lack of social networks, a lack of belonging. Among the things we learn and practice in homes are social rules that protect the common good. "Home" brings a certain space under control (Morley 2000). In homesickness, the nostalgia of home expresses a longing for a particular sense of place and order (Nash 1993). A home is the concretization of a particular moral order. Those people who appear to be home-less fall outside of that moral order. For example, an emergency room doctor writing about his experience with "the homeless" wrestles with the fact that he gave a man $3 (when he could have given him much more) and sent him out into the night when he knew there was no available shelter for him. He asks himself why he didn't do more to help this man and responds:

> Moreover, despite all my attempts to banish it, I still harbor the prejudice that those who cannot sustain themselves in society are less likely to be bound by society's rules. Losing all one's possessions raises the suspicion that a person is somehow out of control in every way. (Ablow 1991, WH9)

The lack of possessions, as opposed to a lack of work, is the fundamental point of alienation—individuals appear to be tied to society through activity as *consumers* and hence as owners of property.

The sense that visibly poor people violate the moral order of capitalism is evidenced by the intense segregation to which they are subjected and also by the kinds of legislation local governments have enacted to control their behavior in public spaces. In Santa Cruz, California, as in many other cities, it is now illegal to sleep in public.[10] In 1994, the city of Santa Cruz also made it illegal to sit on the sidewalk, to tell a lie when panhandling (e.g., to ask for money for food but spend it on cigarettes), and to cover oneself with a blanket or sleeping bag when sitting at night in public space. In 2002, the city of Santa Cruz reconsidered adopting a law that would make it illegal to lean against buildings (McLaughlin 2002). These are public policies directed at people whose very appearance disturbs the notion of public space as communal space and the idealist hope of capitalist prosperity. The visible presence of homeless people violates the sense of commercial shopping areas as centers of belonging and as symbols of capitalist success.

The presence of people living in public spaces violates the notion of public space as an area to move through, not to be in (Bauman 1993). In the United States, to be "homeless" is to be outside of societal order— hence, papers characterize even the ordinary activities of homeless people as different from the ordinary activities of people with housing. For instance, while people with housing live in communities, reporters refer to people who cannot afford housing as living in "encampments" (Toth 1991; Bates 1994; Herman 1982; McMillan 1990). Items as common as sleeping bags become "paraphernalia" (Hill-Holtzman 1992). And, individual efforts of people with housing to directly help poor people are called potentially "foolhardy" (Hubler 1992). To be "homeless" is to be both alien and potentially dangerous.

"Home" functions differently in different social contexts, but it is always connected to discourses about belonging. For instance, if "home" has been a refuge from the world for whites, "homes" in black communities also have been the sites of political resistance (hooks 1992). Discursive practices regarding homelessness are, in many ways, efforts to restore a sense of order. By constituting homeless people as fundamentally alien, and personally responsible for their poverty, the housed public is reassured of their/our own place and possibilities.

The discursive power of homelessness is also produced through the way newspapers assemble information and events regarding people who cannot afford housing as news. Newspapers are generally well-known for producing "first-hand" news stories by interviewing the people involved in any story. It is noteworthy that news articles about homelessness very seldom include the points of view of people who cannot afford housing. In this sense, dominant discourse about homelessness offers wealthier others an escape from knowing about the cultural and personal trauma at the heart of visible poverty. Since the 1990s, papers typically quote women and men *with housing* talking about the presence of "the homeless." This practice is so widely accepted that when papers report "people are tired of homelessness," readers know that "people" refers to those who *have* housing, not those who cannot afford it. Consider:

> "People are tired of homelessness" said a HUD representative. ... "we can't afford the homeless crisis anymore. It's affecting who we are and how we look—and we look terrible." (Shogern 1994, A1)

There is nothing in this article to suggest that the people who are tired of homelessness are those who are living without shelter. Further, newspaper articles often juxtapose "people" with "the homeless," as if these are two distinct groups (cf., Campbell and Reeves 1999). In addition, articles do not quote individuals as housed people per se; rather, articles use the word "we" to imply that the housed person (in this case the HUD representative) being interviewed is speaking for a larger group or community of housed people. The use of "we" is important both in terms of establishing audience identification with the speaker and in terms of placing people who cannot afford housing outside this circle of identification. Individuals who have housing are called to comment on "homelessness" and "the homeless" based on their status as persons living in houses. By quoting housed people, news articles underscore evaluative distinctions between people who can afford housing and those who cannot. In addition, through this practice, news stories elide commonalities—including the fact that many people who cannot afford housing hold jobs.

By standard journalist convention, news articles systematically exclude or disregard people's points of view only in two circumstances: when they are irrelevant, or when the people are believed to be unreliable sources. In order for the journalistic practices that I observed to make sense, those who write and edit articles—as well as those who read them—must take for granted that people who cannot afford housing are either irrelevant to stories about homelessness or that they are unreliable sources of information. In this way, people who cannot afford housing become objects of discourse, rather than subjects of their own experience.

Commercial culture is both a site and resource for "producing, circulating, and enacting" cultural knowledge (Gray 1995b). Discourse about homelessness produces and maintains an understanding of visible poverty as a social problem related to particular kinds of people rather than as an economic problem related to affordable housing, employment, and a living wage. The discursive production of homelessness— as the effect of personal character—begins with, indeed requires, the presumption of an economic meritocracy. In this sense, discourse about homelessness appears to secure, or justify, the economic standing of wealthier others.

The distinction between the causes of poverty and the nature of poor people both relied upon, and produced, an understanding of economic downturns as temporary circumstances from which anyone (like those of us who are living in houses) would soon recover. Because discursive practices personally blame those who fail to recover from economic displacement, discourse about homelessness precludes public discussion of how the trauma of homelessness can produce mental illness and substance abuse that make recovery from poverty almost impossible. In addition, by attributing visible poverty to personal frailties and failures, discursive practices framed "the problem of homelessness" in terms of the difficulties homelessness creates for those who *have* housing. In this way, people with housing become the victims of people who cannot afford housing.

The discursive practices regarding the visible poverty of hundreds of thousands—by some accounts millions—of people belong to a disciplinary discourse, in the Foucaultian sense. The condition of being without housing produces a state of nearly permanent visibility—the ultimate panoptic effect (Foucault 1977) for poor people. But unlike guards in the prison panopticon, those who witness this daily exposure of personal worlds do so unwillingly. The visibility of record numbers of poor people—most of whom are single, white men—seems to have called forth the discourses of alienation that work through "homelessness."

The very personal notion of poverty inherent in discourse about "homelessness" harkens the tales by Horatio Alger that are so popular in the American cultural imagination. The rags-to-riches stories of Horatio Alger are stories of opportunity and hope in which each person achieves according to his or her own ability. More fundamentally, these are stories that depoliticize class inequality by personalizing both poverty and wealth. And it is in this latter sense that the tales of Horatio Alger are quintessentially American. Because Americanness is produced through discourses of equality, democracy, and free competition, the American Dream provokes the social regulation of displays of the wealth and poverty that it produces. The very notion of Americanness is at stake in discourse about people who cannot afford housing—people who remain visibly poor. In this sense "homelessness" is the product of discourses about class struggle that perform a national identity.

A Representational Economy of Self[11]

In this chapter, I examined how people and media engage in practices that actively and systematically disorganize the presence of social and economic capital. At stake in class identities is the capacity for self-recognition (the source of agency) and the capacity of *others* to recognize us—the capacity for collective identities. So it is especially important to note that the very discourses through which people articulated class identities disorganized the presence and meaning of social and economic capital. To the extent that interaction and representation constituted class *as if* it is unrelated to power and wealth, they shrouded the political dimensions of daily life with commonsense knowledge. The discursive production of class obscured the networks of power that emerge through wealth. These networks of power extend beyond resources that are owned to the potential to control both resources and people. And, in this sense the everyday "doing of class" (West and Fenstermaker 1995a), and the discursive formations upon which such doing relies, occluded not only visible displays of wealth and poverty in interaction and representation but also the history and politics of class and class struggle.

Hegemonic discourse effectively subverts the capacity for collective identity based on class interests because class subjects are produced through discourses that conceal class positions, interests, and relationships. Class functions as it does in the United States, not because people are engaged in fictional performances of passing or because they are beset by false consciousness. Rather, class must be understood as performative precisely because discourse—as a kind of societal speech—is a practical part of what people think and feel—how we see the world.

The construction of "middle-classness" *presupposes* the existence of a referent—an imaginary subject, an "average joe" who subsequently becomes real through repetition and interpolation. This is not an analysis of rhetorical practices, but of the imaginary processes through which class is constituted. The constructed historical subject of "the middle class" animates the mythic meanings of class and nation. In this sense, class discourse *performs* a national identity.

The language of class is performative (i.e., constitutive) in that discursive practices produce the relative irrelevance of class that they purport to describe. The relationship between material economic circumstances and the social meanings of those circumstances are not ontologically distinct. While capitalism has always relied on global and local relations of production, it also has produced—and required—particular forms of consciousness. Because relations of exploitation are never lived in economic terms alone, understandings of language in general—and discursive practices in particular—are critical to understanding class struggle. As mentioned at the start of this chapter, we *begin* talking about class within a preexisting discourse shaped by class struggle. Like all hegemonic discursive practices, the discursive production of class secures institutionalized relations of power. One of the most important goals of power is to prevail in determining the agenda of the struggle, to determine which questions can be raised and on what terms. Class conflict is preempted by the hegemonic discursive practices through which class is constituted.

Hegemonic discourse—not material circumstances—shaped class categorizations and subverted the capacity for collective identity/agency based on economic interests. While theories of class offer insight into important aspects of capitalism, within sociology much of this theory is used to reify categories of class and center debates on the adequacy and limitations of various categorization efforts. However, even if one thinks of class in purely economic terms, it exceeds existing frameworks for understanding class. Is it reasonable to think of someone with $450,000 in assets as wealthy? What if those assets are equity accrued through forty years of real estate inflation on a small house owned by someone who works in a small factory making jewelry? How is one to understand the class position of a person who earns $70,000 a year as an independent contractor in the technology industry and who is unable to afford to buy a home because of inflated housing prices? If working-class jobs once provided workers and others with the ability to buy not only homes and cars but also boats and vacation property, this is no longer the case. Today, even people with upper-income professional careers do not necessarily experience the benefits of what was once considered wealth; rather, many now refer to themselves as "house poor" because all of their income is tied up in homeownership. This is not to equate those who are "house poor" with those who are living on minimum wage in a rented apartment, but to argue that historical categories of class are inadequate for understanding the contemporary distribution of wealth, the kinds of work and remuneration available, and the potential for social justice organizing. We are in need of new epistemologies for conceptualizing class.

Understanding how identity and subjectivity are constituted within language and representation provides an opportunity to retheorize economic inequalities and the possibilities for social change. The imagined communities of class are not distinguished by truth or falsity but by the styles in which they are imagined which allow us to recognize different parts of our histories, and to construct points of identification. If discourse produces classed subjects, the *dialogic* relationship between identity and subjectivity organizes a self. Through the dialogic relationship between identity and subjectivity, people unable to afford housing come to be "the homeless" as opposed, for instance, to "bums" or "vagrants." Disindentification requires and produces changes in how we see the world—gives us another imaginary with which to think. Consider, for instance, simply beginning to talk about people who cannot afford housing. Translate news stories about homeless bashing into stories of assaults on people who cannot afford housing. The later formulation reconstitutes what is covered-over in the first. And it is this kind of reconstitution that is crucial to the transformation of public discourse as well as to the transformation of social and material relations.

The work of disindentification requires resituating the politics that personalize poverty and wealth into the historical conditions that make each possible and apparently natural. This would require the re-membering of self and others by calling into question the identities we have come to inhabit as members of a "classless" nation. As scholars, one means through which we can advance an agenda of social justice is by working at the constitutive frontiers of language to imagine new socialities, new subjectivities. In the beginning of the twenty-first century, resistance to hegemonic economic forces in the United States requires an understanding of the performativity of language in relation to material conditions lived experience.

5

MOVING FORWARD

While there are many forms of culturally specific commonsense knowledge, the analyses of this book have taken up some of the ways in which shared cultural assumptions about race, gender, and class link people together across these very same categories of difference—often in ways that unintentionally perpetuate and extend inequalities. The theoretical, methodological, and interpretative strategies brought to bear on media and interviews have offered an analytical framework for examining both the production of "difference" and ways to challenge those productions. Throughout, I have attempted to demonstrate how individual practices articulate cultural processes and how cultural processes produce the conditions that constitute local practices. In short, my analytical focus has concerned, not the contents of experience, but the *processes* of experience. In this brief chapter I examine the productive force of language and implications for social research and social change.

The constitutive force of language, through which we become both individuals and members of communities, is inherently moral, producing not only identity but also difference. Less clear perhaps has been an understanding of how, or where, to locate the generative power of language. Based on analyses in this book, it might seem accurate to say that the generative power of language derived from the ability of a single expression, or representation, to articulate multiple discourses. Recall the discourse of gender that, not only produced a world of beings who appeared to be naturally women and men—but also produced heterosexuality, homophobia, racism, xenophobia, classism, and citizenship.

The disciplinary power of gender discourse became visible through the subjects it produced. The generative force of language was anchored through a multiplicity of sites and a repetition of strategies. Recall also the numerous repetitions of heterosexuality within a brief television scene in *Judging Amy*, and the circulation of repetitions across television shows, newspaper articles, and interviews. The circulation and repetition of discourses extends even further, reaching both back through history and forward into the future. Because knowledge/power travels across time, it can never be wholly produced in a local context; consequently, the constitutive force of language needs to be understood through its ability to travel. However, to speak of the constitutive force of language is meaningless without the context of local practices.

The power of discursive formations depends on some aspect of human agency in a local context. Discourses gain their materiality in local contexts. Consequently, it would be incorrect to attribute the vast power of language exclusively to either agency (human or otherwise) or to discourses. Discourse is what Derrida (1982) called an "exergue" in relation to studies of talk. That is to say, discourse is both outside the immediacy of talk and the face of the coin upon which talk is stamped. Precisely because of this complexity, no single analytical paradigm will ever fully comprehend or articulate the complexities that pass without notice everyday.

The relationship between human agency and discursive power is inherently unstable. Using tools from ethnomethodology and post-structural discourse analysis provides a means with which to trace fluid networks of knowledge/power within and beyond local contexts. For instance, by analyzing the discursive production of race, I was able to demonstrate how the apparent incoherence of race actually strengthens the stability of racial categories in daily life. Ethnomethodological tools provided a means to apprehend the local effects of discursive power and the ways that people advanced and resisted power. Only in local contexts can strategies emerge for challenging hegemonic relations. Developing more, and different, sociological analyses of language can provide a rich basis for reexamining and retheorizing how categories of social difference continue to exist as effective tools of exploitation.

Like the boundaries in everyday life, the boundaries of sociological theory and methods presuppose a point of view. Nor are disciplinary boundaries neutral, but, rather, inherently political. By transgressing the boundaries between social sciences and the humanities, I have attempted to illustrate the multiple levels on which power can operate and the variety of means through which power can be constrained in order to develop a multidimensional analysis of culture, knowledge, and power. By engaging analyses of discourse with local analyses of talk, I have tried to create understandings of race, gender, and class that do not dislocate knowledge/power from their production.

Ethnomethodology and poststructural discourse analysis provide analytical strategies that do not dismiss race, gender, and class as linguistic phantoms, but rather, provide a means to critically engage both the practices and the hegemonic discursive formations through which such categories are produced. By drawing from each it is possible to develop analyses that refuse the classically antithetical relationship between equality and difference, in which "sameness is the only ground on which equality can be claimed" (Scott 1988, 174). Race, gender, and class only exist meaningfully within discourses and practices about them. On what terms and under what circumstances do these categories convene and fall apart? How can discourses of race and gender be deployed for cross-class alliances? This book leaves more to be explored and elaborated upon. "Because *we and the people and things we choose to study* are routinely both producing and awash in seas of discourses, analyzing only individual and collective human actors no long suffices for many qualitative projects" (italics in the original; Clarke 2005, 145). It is essential to cultivate new analytical frameworks and methodological strategies to understand how constitutive processes and material resources are reflexively related.

The analyses in this book may seem to be irrelevant to the needs of the most marginal in society, such as those who live in severe poverty and/or with survival-level concerns. Enormous differences among daily concerns, both around the globe and within the United States, amplify existing debates between poststructural and material feminisms. While survival-level needs will rarely be directly addressed by any social theory, this does not mean that theory is irrelevant. Consider for instance, theories of rape are of no use to a woman being raped, but this does not dismiss the importance of voluminous feminist scholarship on rape—both for those who have faced rape and for those who have not. The usefulness of social theory will never be measured by its ability to contain violence in the moment but by its ability to provide strategies that can prevent the violence from repeating. Careful examination of the processes through which inequality and difference are made to appear inevitable and overpowering is never irrelevant to the lives of those who are most marginalized.

To register the possibilities of democratic action it is necessary to move beyond the limiting methodological, theoretical, and disciplinary positions that present dichotomous binaries of macro and micro, culture and politics, discourse and agency, social inequalities and daily practice. To move beyond these frameworks is to rethink relations among culture, knowledge, and power in an effort to reconstruct democracy.

From the Bottom Up

Poststructural discourse analysis is not an attempt to escape the materiality of bodies but an effort to relocate the production of that materiality in the larger context of discursive formations of power/knowledge. In this respect, this book has presented a mapping that can lead to understanding both continuity and difference. The unities that categories of race, gender, and class seem to proclaim are constructed through the play of power and exclusion; consequently, such categories of subjectivity and identity are not an inevitable or primordial totality but are the result of the naturalized, and overdetermined process of "closure" (Bhabha cited in Hall 1996, 5).[1]

All systems of classification are generative in that they produce both meanings and order—hence, classification must also be understood as a system of power, but not inherently so. While systems of classification distinguish between this and that, say between a ball and an apple, social contexts provide the means for interpreting or ranking the importance of each category (cf., Hall 1997a). The ball may be more important on a playground, the apple more important in the grocery bag. The *repetition* of local contexts, in which objects are constituted repeatedly through a hierarchical ranking, leads to power relations that extend beyond any individual context. This is why analyses of local contexts can never, in themselves, adequately account for relations of power—and why they are also essential to the theorization of power. While a ball, an apple, gender, and race are all categories of classifications, their relative importance as categories—as systems of classifications—depends upon, not only their use in a particular context, but their repetition over time in *multiple* local contexts. An analysis of commonsense knowledge is critical to demonstrating how daily practices enunciate relationships to the historical world. In addition, commonsense knowledge reveals how a vernacular moral order is sustained through multiple repetitions in multiple contexts, which collectively produce that which is ordinary and that which is denied ordinariness.

The geographies of difference in the twentieth-first century call for performative strategies that refuse cultural, historical, and biological forms of essentialism. Such strategies are possible only by constantly critiquing the terms by which "difference" becomes visible and meaningful. My analyses demonstrate some of the ways in which reality is constituted through an imaginary. This is not to say people inhabit fantasy worlds that do not exist, but that we constantly create both the meanings of our experiences and the categories of existence. To analyze how all people are implicated in the processes of oppression and exploitation does not deny the effects of systematic oppression and exploitation—it relocates sources of power and agency. This yields at least two, related forms of resistance: disidentification and what Butler (1996, 377) refers to as "strategic provisionality." Both of these require taking stock of the discourses through which subjectivities are produced, and then reimagining oneself differently.

Strategies of disidentification refuse *assumptions* of shared interests within categories and seek instead to understand the conditions of emergence that give rise both to the immediate problem and attendant productions of "difference." This means that under certain conditions, African Americans may have more political commonality with some Native Americans than with other African Americans. Puerto Ricans may have more in common with the political struggles of Native Hawaiians than with Latinos. Yet it is not only a matter of recognizing the commonality, but also on that basis, refusing and making visible the relations of power that hegemonic discourse would conceal.

By contrast, strategic provisionality is an organizational strategy that invokes hegemonic identity categories while at the same time avowing the contingency of them. Such a critical engagement requires a strategic use of categories that maintain a reflexive analysis of the circumstances of its own constitution. At times, it is most effective to organize as "women," "lesbians," "Latinos," or "poor people." But using these identifications as a strategic provisionality prevents closure—prevents the once and for all statement that says this is what it means to be a woman, a lesbian, Latino, or poor. Strategic provisionality uses the signs of social categories to subvert the hegemonic repetitions that fix or essentialize identities. Most importantly, strategic provisionality deprives categories of their putative descriptive power by revealing both their contingencies and constitutive power. To talk about disidentification and strategic provisionality is to shift from a notion of fixed identity (and through them, identity politics) to discussion of identifications.

Unlike identities which appear—at least to a commonsense view—to be stable and coherent, identifications are constructed through recognitions and as such are processes rather than modes of being (Hall 1996). As *processes*, identifications are always contingent; hence, once an identification is made, it does not obliterate "difference" but rather operates across difference both transgressing and marking edges (Hall 1996, 3).

Identifications, then, mark the points of attachment that reflect not only a vision of history but also a rupture in the articulation of history that opens to a different vision of the future. Hence, Balibar (2002) urges us to speak of identifications and processes of identification as a way of acknowledging that while identities can be fixed, no identity is inherently or permanently existent. Identifications then defy commonsense.

Because identification is always an ambivalent process—we never fully identify with any single interpellation—interpellation can never precisely constitute a subject. Butler (1977b) asserts that this ambivalence enables the possibility, not of refusing, but of reworking the very terms of becoming a subject. In addition, since matrices of discourse interpellate subjects through repetitions over time, the subject is neither spoken into existence, nor produced in its totality, at an instant. Although the subject is produced through repetition, it is not produced anew again and again—but neither is it produced exactly the same each time. Thus the process of repetition can undermine the normalizing force of interpellation (Butler 1997c, 93). Because subjects are created repeatedly, differently, and in different circumstances, the possibilities of resistance, nonconformity, and variation become possible. And finally, while interpellation creates a *social* being by naming, one need not respond in order to be interpellated. Here again, there is potential slippage between how we are seen and how we see ourselves. Identifications and disidentifications become fluid ways of negotiating a social geography in which it is increasingly difficult to think of social identities as "human nature." The lack of an inherently existent human nature energizes the possibilities for change, rather than fixing the possibilities of existence.

Revisiting the Sociological Imagination

The analytical framework of this book attempted to demonstrate the importance of connecting local productions of gender, race, and class to each other and to broader cultural contexts of knowledge/power. Clearly, this pushes the boundary of sociological inquiry. Glyn Williams (1999, 294) argues that

> Sociology's emergence as a feature of modernism was responsible for the separation of language, mind, and reality. This meant that it was possible to study reality without reference to language. It also meant that reality was reflected in language and that a consideration of evidence, as language, implied an introduction to truth. In the same manner, language and nature were separated, involving the separation of representation and fact. This meant that society could become something to study, as

something separate from language. In a sense language was excluded from proto-sociology.

Concerned with notions of empirical evidence, studies of language in sociology have been produced technical analyses of talk—for example, conversation analysis and sociolinguistics—rather than interpretative studies of language. My own research owes much to ethnomethodology, even as it marks a radical departure. Social scientists in general, and sociologist in particular, will likely continue to disagree about the place of language in sociological studies. Since the possibility of agency and the potential for change exists only in the "everydayness" of living, studies of agency must be grounded in local, material contexts. Recall that in Chapter 2 by focusing analyses of race *only* on local contexts of talk and interaction, the various ways of conceptualizing race as culture, color, blood, and nation could appear to be incongruous, if not contradictory. However, if the constitutive effects of language are examined only in interactional terms, they are dislocated from the broader contexts of place and time (Gubrium and Holstein 1997). Key aspects of privilege are produced as tangible effects that do not leave a trail of evidence to analyze; the production of systematic erasures do not leave quotes to analyze. Without analyses of discourse, it is impossible to comprehend the production of erasures and cultural contexts. At the same time, theoretical analysis of discourse often occlude the daily practices through which people *participate* in reproducing discourses and normalizing their effects. Because commonsense knowledge links the local production of meanings to the cultural production of knowledge, it provides a key focal point for examining the dialogical relationship between the apparent agency of local practices and the efficacy of cultural discourse.

The schism between studies of talk and theories of language prevents a full analysis of knowledge, power, and agency. More and different forms of studies of language are needed precisely because all meaning is produced through language and so it is through a study of language that we can see the processes which constitute the presence, meaning, and value of social life. Sociological analyses of language are not just a matter of interpreting former questions differently, or of interpreting "evidence" differently. More importantly, sociological studies of language allow us to ask questions that have been previously foreclosed. It is not just that there has been disagreement about the kinds of problems sociology can solve, but that existing standards and paradigms have made particular kinds of problems impossible to legitimately investigate. The robustness of sociology is dependent upon its ability to allow for a variety of analytical paradigms and explorations. Studies of language illuminate inequalities differently—by drawing the weight of history into the local production of meaning and the interpretation of lived experience—and hence offer new strategies for social justice.

APPENDIX A

INTERVIEWEES

Name	Age	Sex	Education	Self-identified	Employment	Appx. Income	Appx. Assets
Charles Adams	49	M	H.S.	White	None/ Homeless	0	None
Captain Ahab	53	M	MA/JD	Caucasian	Attorney	$200,000	$500,000
Marisol Alegria	62	F	B.S.	Hispanic	Franchise Owner	$250,000	$10,000,000
Peter Alford	45	M	B.A.	African American	Letter Carrier	$100,000	$500,000
Brady	56	M	J.D.	White	Attorney	$250,000	$5,000,000
Charlie Chin	56	M	M.B.A.	Chinese American	Land & Business Developer	$200,000	$10,000,000
Cuautehmoc	24	M	Junior H.S.	Mexican	Retail Clerk	$15,000	None
Lorraine Doe	45	F	M.A.	American Indian	Counselor/ Tribal Administrator	$200,000	$500,000,000
Nikki Drew	42	F	2 Years College	White	None/ Homeless	0	None
Lana Jacobs	59	F	Junior College	Black	Artist	$100,000	$1,000,000
Lue Lani	71	F	College	White	Real Estate (Sales)	$40,000	$500,000
Zach Mauro	47	M	A.A.	Filipino	Package Driver	$60,000	$250,000

-continued

Name	Age	Sex	Education	Self-identified	Employment	Appx. Income	Appx. Assets
Sherry Moss	57	F	Junior H.S.	White	None/Homeless	0	None
Polard Parker	50	M	B.A.	White	Real Estate (Developer)	$500,000	$100,000,000
Emerson Piscopo	33	F-M	2 Years College	Italian/ Caucasian	Stylist/Colorist	$45,000	(Unclear)
Lucy Rogers	43	F	D.C.	Latina	Chiropractor	$80,000	$250,000
Rudy Rosales	53	M	H.S.	American Indian	Retired Laborer	$40,000	None
Ann-Marie Sayers	51	F	--	Native American	Tribal Chair/ (Foundation) Director	$50,000	There is no value placed on Indian Canyon
Anglico Simon	30	M	H.S./ EMT	Caucasian	Delivery Driver	$50,000	None
Betty Sukarai	23	F	B.A.	Japanese American	Teller/Loan Officer	$30,000	$100,000
Roberta Washington	65	F	H.S.	Negro	Cashier	$10,000	None
Ashley Worthington	30	M-F	B.A.	White/ Caucasian	Web Designer/ Marketer	$60,000	None
Brownie Wu	68	F	Some College	Chinese American	Retail Clerk	$90,000	$500,000

APPENDIX B

COLLECTION OF NEWSPAPER ARTICLES

I devised a search of newspaper articles by first locating papers that use the same indexing system for their stories. This research provided my initial search base: the *Los Angeles Times,* the *New York Times,* the *Washington Post,* the *Christian Science Monitor,* and the *Wall Street Journal.* The indices for these papers covered the fifteen-year period of 1982 through 1996 (the year I began collecting data). I then conducted a keyword search for news stories containing the words (or variations on the words) homeless, vagrant(s), streetpeople, or transient(s). This keyword produced a database of 4,814 articles. I narrowed the scope of the research to the *Los Angeles Times,* the *Washington Post,* and the *New York Times* because these papers are widely read and also because the articles which appear in them are often reprinted in smaller, local papers. Consequently, their ability to influence journalistic conventions as well as what counts as news is quite significant. This reduced my database to 3,789 articles. Beginning with the second article in this collection, I randomly selected every seventh article; I then eliminated all articles that referred to countries other than the United States and to homelessness resulting from natural disasters such as floods, fires, and earthquakes. I restricted my search to incidence of homelessness among people who cannot afford permanent shelter because there are substantive qualitative differences between temporary homelessness caused by a natural disaster and that caused by chronic poverty. The responses of people in the United States toward those without housing demonstrate categorical distinctions between those unable to afford housing and those displaced by natural disaster (Pascale 1995). The final data set was composed of 413 articles: 251 from the *New York Times,* 75 from the *Los Angeles Times,* and 87 from the *Washington Post.* (My data include a disproportionate number of newspaper articles from the *New York Times,* because the *New York Times* produces a disproportionate number of articles.)

ENDNOTES

Chapter 1

1. Throughout, I use the word "discourse" to refer to "clusters of ideas, images, and practices" that provide frameworks for understanding what knowledge is useful, relevant, and true in any given context (Hall 1997c, 6). Discourses establish frames of intelligibility through a series of processes and relationships; consequently discursive analyses examine the procedures through which the frames of intelligibility are produced (Foucault 1972).
2. The term ethnomethodology, invented by Harold Garfinkel, literally means "people's methods." Ethnomethodology arose as a critique of what Garfinkel saw as mainstream sociology's tendency to treat people as "cultural dopes," who need sociologists to explain how the world works. Ethnomethodology begins with the premise that social life as an ongoing interactional accomplishment and provides tools for understanding the continual sense-making practices that pass without notice in daily life.
3. Functionally overdetermined refers to analyses that collapse, or fail to account for, multiple and/or contradictory processes that contribute to a single event or circumstance. Rather, the complexity of contributory factors is displaced by a focus is an apparently singular factor or process. The roots of this term can be traced from Freud to Althusser, and Baudrillard.
4. The network of beliefs about the nature of reality, self, and other that passes as commonsense (Garfinkel 1967) has also been referred to as the "thesis of the natural standpoint" (Husserl 1962), *préjugé du monde* (Merleau-Ponty 1964) and mundane reason (Pollner 1987).
5. Through moral discourses we learn who we are, to whom we are connected, and what matters enough to care about and care for (Walker 1998, 201). Consider how colonialism centered two moral discourses: one of propagating "civilization" and the other, affirming the inequality of human races and the right of the strong to dominate the weak (Todorov 1995).
6. Functionalism is a sociological theory that posits social institutions as a stable and integrated system that meets the social needs of society's members. Within functionalism society is likened to a human body in which all of the parts "function" for the good of the whole. This emphasis on social cohesion is often criticized for an inability to adequately address social conflict and change.

7. Later studies on the social construction of deviance departed from this functionalist legacy. For research on language and the social construction of putatively moral concerns see Gusfield (1975) on drunk driving, Schneider (1978) on alcoholism, Rose's (1977) analysis of rape, as well as Markel (1979) and Schneider (1984) on smoking. More recently, sociologists (cf., Bellah 1991, 1996; Childs 1998; Lamont 1992) have taken up constructionist analyses of moral and ethical values within and across societies.

8. Todorov (1995) and Eze (1997) also develop this line of thought through analyses that link Western moral theory to ideologies of cultural supremacy and whiteness.

9. Hegemony is never a permanent state of affairs, and never uncontested. Hall (1980) writes that "hegemony is always the temporary mastery of a particular theater of struggle. It marks a shift in the dispositions of contending forces in a field of struggle and the articulation of that field into a tendency. Such tendencies do not immediately 'profit' a ruling class or a fraction of capital, but they create the conditions whereby society and the state may be conformed in a larger sense to certain formative national-historical tasks. Thus the particular outcomes always depend on the balance in the relations of force in any theater of struggle and reform.... Its effect is to show how cultural questions can be linked in a non-reductionist manner, to other levels: it enables us to think of societies as complex formations, necessarily contradictory, always historically specific" (36).

10. "The assumption of an objective world, a determinant order 'out there,' dialectically implicates a network of other distinctions. The 'objective out there,' for example implies a 'subjective in-here.' It implies as well certain modalities through which individuals may experience reality such as 'perception' or observation' and modalities in which individuals turn from the real to the subjective as in 'imagination,' 'hallucination,' or 'dreams'" (Pollner 1987, 21).

11. I am indebted to Umberto Eco's (1998) inspiration in this line of thinking.

12. Analytic induction forms the foundation of grounded theory, the basis of symbolic interactionism, and several varieties of CDA, as well as less interpretive forms of sociology. Despite this methodological commonality, each of these forms of analyses relies on different epistemologies, logic, and literatures. Importantly, each understands the relationship between individuals and social structures in significantly different ways.

13. Discourse analysis developed in the United Kingdom as a critique of scientific knowledge (cf., Gilbert and Mulkay 1984). In this paradigm, discourse refers to the texts and talk through which disciplinarity is produced; people are understood to be active agents who use discourses to achieve objectives. Discourse analysis examines rhetoric, metaphor, and figures of speech; it focuses on the persuasive character of discourse—understood more denotatively as written or spoken communication. Although developed within the U.K., the sociology of scientific knowledge has flourished in the United States in social psychology where it gained a more empirically-grounded methodology (Wooffitt 2005). It is possible that the lack of detailed methodology for doing discourse analysis made it a poor match for the demands of U.S. sociology where ethnomethodology and conversation analysis provide if not the sole, certainly the primary, resources for studying texts and talk.

14. Studies of language in sociology also include a focus on sociolinguistics pioneered by Joshua Fishman and often referred to as the sociology of language. This line of scholarship has more marginal influence in American sociology.

15. Because ethnomethodology and symbolic interactionism share an analytical focus on interaction, their approaches are often mistaken as being the same. While a meaningful comparison exceeds the limits of this book, most simply, they can be differentiated by their orientations toward social structures and toward language

and interaction. Symbolic interaction is rooted in an ontology that is consistent with Weber and Durkheim (Maines 1977). Hence, symbolic interactionism understands social structures as an existing *context* for interaction. Further, it examines the relationships between people and structures through analyses of symbolic communication and action. By contrast, for ethnomethodologists, social structures are *processes* to be understood through the social interactions that reflexively constitute them. The ethnomethodological concern with the production of meaning in interaction demands a narrowly focused analytical context, which does not regard social structures in the abstract, as either empowering or constraining forces. In addition, language and interaction are constitutive elements that produce an apparently objective social world; they are not symbolic practices of meaning-making such as can be found in labeling theory.

16. Garfinkel's study of Agnes' accomplishment of gender remains controversial and marked by strong criticism (Denzin 1990, 1991) and a corresponding defense (Hilbert 1991; Maynard 1991).

17. Sacks and Schegloff later elaborated on the concepts of accounts and accountability through development of conversation analysis.

18. Those categories for which one may be held account-able must be relevant to the membership categories in play in the immediate context. For example, consider that a family is composed of members such as parents, children, cousins, aunts, and uncles. Therefore within a family one may be called to account for her or his behavior *as* a parent, a child, a cousin, etc. In environments in which gender is a relevant membership category, one may be called upon to "act like a man" or "to be a lady" (cf., West 1987). Anomie is a situation in which any account will do, or no account will do (Hilbert 1992, 96).

19. Denzin (1990), for example, is critical that such a practice can produce more than "selective objectivity," while Woolgar and Pawluch (1985) characterize such practice as "ontological gerrymandering," that is to say exempting one's own research practices from the analytics brought to bear on the accounts of others. Indeed, it would seem impossible to write an analysis that is fully engaged and completely self-reflexive.

20. Critical discourse analysis draws from sociolinguistics to examine the order and organization of communication to produce analyses of ideologies, power, and inequalities. CDA takes up, in addition to linguistic analysis, analytic categories that are not manifest in the transcript under study but nonetheless are argued to provide a broader sociopolitical context for the interaction. The solid linguistic basis of CDA includes sentence structure, syntax, and verb tense and incorporates a broadly Marxist perspective (Fairclough 1992, 1995; Fairclough and Wodak 1997). However, there is no single methodological or theoretical focus to CDA. Indeed CDA analysts mediate between the linguistic and the social by drawing a variety of scholars and paradigms including Aristotle and the continental philosophers, as well as Althusser, Barthes, Gramsci, Foucault, Pecheux, Marxism, the Frankfurt school, neo-Marxism, the Centre for Contemporary Cultural Studies (including Stuart Hall), deconstruction, and postmodernism. Particularly in social-psychology, CDA has been influenced by ethnomethodology, conversation analysis, sociology of scientific knowledge (also referred to as discourse analysis) poststructural discourse analysis, communication, linguistic philosophy, and rhetoric (Wood and Kroger 2000). Further, scholars such as Threadgold (1997) inflect critical discourse analysis with distinctly feminist concerns and analyses. For a more detailed lineage see Billig (2003), Van Dijik (1993), Weiss and Wodak (2003), Wetherell, Taylor and

Yates (2001), Wodak (2001), and Wood and Kroger (2000). Given the richness of these influences one might begin to imagine the diversity of analytical frameworks within CDA. Indeed it is possible to have two books on CDA analysis, both on the same topic, but with little or no overlap.

The variations of CDA are both inter- and intra-disciplinary, inter- and intra-national. For example, there are distinctions between CDA in the U.K. (cf., Fairclough 1997; Wetherell and Potter 1987), the Vienna school (cf., Wodak 2001), the more cognitive approach of Dutch CDA (cf., Van Dijik 1993, 1997) and the Duisberg school (which consists work by Siefried Jäger and, for the most part, is not yet translated into English). See Wood and Kroger 2000, 213–216 for a partial comparison of CDA styles and Van Dijk 1993 for an overview.

While the heterogeneity of CDA as a transdisciplinary field of study has produced dynamic and fluid research, the variety of theoretical and methodological orientations within CDA also has produced a lack defining analytic coherence as well as multiple and conflicting epistemologies and nomenclatures, which often produce conflicting notions of agency and subjectivity. For instance, while laying claim to the constitutive nature of discourse, researchers will also characterize discourse as an intentional activity. According to Wodak and colleagues (1999, 8), "Through discourses, social actors constitute objects of knowledge, situations and social roles as well as identities and interpersonal relations between different social groups and those who interact with them." Discourse, therefore, appears to gain constitutive power through the intention and agency of persons—quite the opposite of poststructural conceptions of discourse. Even when CDA research explicitly lays claims to Foucaudian and poststructural analyses, researchers write about discourse as the *carrier* of ideology (cf., Fairclough 1997; Reisigl and Wodak 2001). In this sense, CDA produces insights into communication and ideology and, consequently, shares an ontology and epistemology that is more consistent with Althuser and Pêcheux than with poststructuralists such as Derrida or Butler. In addition, the CDA research that draws from postmodern and poststructural theory often is marked by an "inconsistent application of key aspects" of the relevant theories (Hepburn 1997, 30). Some CDA research does use discourse in ways that seem to be more consistent with French poststructuralism (cf., Hepburn 1997).

21. "While ethnomethodologists have traditionally been interested in local practices of enactment, they have generally been reluctant to explicitly engage the challenge posed by the recurrence of patterned interpretations. Interpretation is certainly 'artful' (Garfinkel 1967), but it also produces and reproduces categorizations that are recognizable as instances of the same phenomenon. Interpretative practice attaches meaning to occurrence in familiar ways. That sense of familiarity, of course, is not merely a matter of recognition; it, too, is artfully accomplished" (Holstein and Miller 1993, 153).

By comparison, in CDA, Wetherell (1998) draws from Laclau and Mouffe to argue for the analytical power of incorporating conversation analysis with poststructural analysis asserting that by making reference only to that which can be empirically demonstrated, leads to an impoverished and politically naïve view of social life. In addition, with regard to symbolic interaction, scholars (Clarke 2005; Denzin 2001; Dunn 1997) have argued for sociological studies that combine symbolic interaction with poststructural analyses in order to connect local and broader cultural contexts.

22. Some ethnomethodologists have begun to explore the relationship of extra-textual material to their analyses (Watson and Seiler 1992). These studies demonstrate a variety of ways in which researchers have drawn from ethnomethodology to better understand relationships among language, knowledge, power, and talk. Although the approaches in this collection are quite varied, these explorations expand upon the ethnomethodological assertion that "while there is nothing but the text, not everything needed for its analysis is in the text" (Watson and Seiler 1992, XV). Among the ethnomethodological analyses that include an expanded notion of local context are Hak's (1992) study of psychiatric records, which concludes such records cannot be completely defined or analyzed locally since the records must bear some relation to "ideal" psychiatric competence and Bjelic and Lynch's (1992) study, which concludes that to understand Newton's and Geothe's theories of prismatic color, it is essential examine both the physical and discursive processes of experimentation that generated each of the theories. Heap's (1992) study of collaborative computer editing, and Hester's (1992) study of student "deviance" each conclude that, for study participants to understand their activities and conversations, they needed to refer to a background of normative resources; consequently this background needed to be made explicit. Drawing from a conversation analysis of mishearings, Blimes (1992) concludes that cultural and biographical knowledge, as well as situational contexts, are essential to understanding conversation. In addition, Dorothy Smith (1990a, 1990b, 1999) draws from ethnomethodology to establish tools for the methodological investigation of the social organization of knowledge and power as evidenced in concrete situations.

23. Social sciences initially adopted the surveying term "triangulation" as a metaphor for covergent validation (Campbell 1956; Campbell and Fiske 1959 in Berg 2007, 6). Although triangulation in the social sciences initially referred to using more than one research method to analyze a single phenomenon, more recently, it has come to refer to strategies that deploy not only multiple methods but also those which increase validity through the use of multiple theories, multiple researchers, and/or multiple data sets (Berg 2007; Denzin 1989; Punch 2005). Further, triangulation can refer to within-method triangulation and between-method triangulation (Berg 2007). Modes of triangulation are not equivalent in terms of their complexity, strengths, or weaknesses, but rather that each is thought to provide a potentially more comprehensive picture of the social world than any single method might.

24. Triangulation often is criticized as a metaphor that goes too far in creating a misplaced certainty about the social world, for regarding data sets derived from different methods as equivalent in their capacity to address the research question; and, for the implicit assumption of a fixed social reality. For further reading see Moran-Ellis et al. (2006) and Punch (2005) and Silverman (2004). Many fine critiques of this form of science currently exist in general (cf., Haraway 1991; Harding 1991; Latour 1993) and of triangulation as a method of validity in particular (cf., Miller and Fox 2004; Saukko 2003).

25. Suzanne Kessler (2001) credits Virginia Prince with coining the term "transgender" in 1979 to describe her decision "to become a woman without changing her genitals."

26. I am indebted to conversations with Salvador Vidal-Ortiz for this line of thinking.

Chapter 2

1. As social inquiry made a transition from philosophy to social science, August Comte shaped sociology as a science, in part by introducing the term positivism, which limited research to matters that could be directly tested, and therefore distinguished sociology from philosophy and aligned it with existing science. Within sociology positivism came to express a style of inquiry associated with quantitative analyses of putatively objective conditions and essential natures.

2. Critical studies in whiteness produced important changes in how race could be studied and understood but did not, in the same sense, yield a paradigmatic shift.

3. For earlier studies of racial accountability see West (1995a, b, 1999).

4. Throughout, I have transcribed words in capital letters to indicate a spoken emphasis. I use ellipses to indicate spoken pauses and ellipses in brackets to indicate where I edited the quotation. I place my own comments for clarification in brackets. In addition, I include nonverbal components of communication such as long pauses and clearing one's throat. These notations are not as complex as those used in conversation analysis but are similarly intended to provide a fuller context for readers.

5. It is worth noting that despite the surprise and sarcasm of my interviewees when I asked about their racial identities, I was able to pose the question without ever compromising my competence as a researcher—unlike the correlate question: Do you have a gender identity? Which so badly compromised my standing as a "serious" researcher that I could not pose the question without troubling the interview.

6. The UPI manual goes on to note that in stories that involve a conflict, it is important "to specify that an issue cuts across racial lines. If, for example, a demonstration by supporters of busing to achieve racial balance in schools includes a substantial number of whites, that fact should be noted" (UPI 1992, 236). The *Washington Post Style Manual* advises journalists that race may be relevant in stories involving politics, social action, social conditions, achievement, and other matters where race can be a distinguishing factor; where usage has sanctioned the description such as a black leader, Irish tenor, Polish wedding; and when reporting an incident that cannot be satisfactorily explained without reference to race (Webb, 1978, 35). Additionally, the *Washington Post* style manual specifies that "the mere fact tha[t] an incident involves persons of different races does not, of itself, mean that racial tags should be used. And when racial identification is used, the races of all involved should be mentioned" (Webb, 1978, 35).

7. In a later section of this chapter, I examine commonsense knowledge in relationship to the multiple meanings of race that circulate in public discourse.

8. Pêcheux (1982, 156–159) delineated disindentification as one of three mechanisms through which subjects may be constructed. Identification is the mode of the 'good' subject who consents, that is to say, the subject identifies with the discursive formation that dominates him or her (Pêcheux 1982, 187). Counter-identification is the mode of the 'trouble-makers' who turn back the meanings, by saying for example "what *you call* the oil crisis," "*your* social sciences," "*your* Virgin Mary." The rejection is in some ways still complicit with the production of the identity.

9. Betty's elaboration of the food and rituals that came from the Japanese side of her family demonstrates both what it means to her to be "half anything" and more broadly the logic of multiculturalism in which racial difference enriches white culture through food and arts. This conception of multiculturalism embraces "difference" stripped of history and power.

10. This news segment concerned potential regulation of the pharmaceutical industry aimed at reducing the cost of prescription drugs to senior citizens.

11. In 1897 a federal court in Texas admitted Rodriguez, a Mexican, to citizenship and noted that by anthropological terms he would "probably not" be classified as white (López 1996, 61). More recently, some legal scholars have tried to frame Mexican identity as racial, rather than cultural, to secure protection from discrimination (López 1996, 125–126).

12. It is important to note that this kind of slippage in the production of race is possible only with respect to people with light skin tones.

13. Importantly, the difference between a black subject passing as white and a white subject passing as white is not an essential difference, but a structural difference that demonstrates that "passing involves the re-staging of a fractured history of identifications that constitute the limits" of a subject's mobility (Ahmed 1999, 93).

Chapter 3

1. Kessler and McKenna (1978) argue that members use a basic schema for making gender attributions, which is to see someone as female only when you cannot see them as male. They further assert that the sex/gender distinction falsely preserves the notion that sex is based on purely biological criteria. "[W]e not only create gender as a construct, but we create the specific categories 'female' and 'male.' We must be doing more than gender; we must be doing *male* or *female* gender" (emphasis in the original, Kessler and McKenna 1978, 155). Hence, Kessler and McKenna use "gender" even when referring to those aspects of being women and men that traditionally have been viewed as biological. By using the term "gender" in place of "sex," Kessler and McKenna (1978) attempt to highlight the social processes that produce the appearance of biological status. By contrast West and Zimmerman (1987) elaborated on distinctions between sex (assigned on the basis of socially agreed upon biological criteria), sex category, and gender. For instance, Agnes (Garfinkel 1967), as a transsexual, sustained her claim to being female through more than gendered activities (i.e., feminine behavior); she had to make herself *categorically* recognizable as female (West and Zimmerman 1987). This distinction between behavior that is accountable to sex category membership and those qualities that make individuals recognizable as women or as men is central to "doing gender" (Fenstermaker, West, and Zimmerman 1991; West and Fenstermaker 1995a; West and Zimmerman 1987).

2. According to Butler (1993), sex is something of a fiction because it is a site to which there is no direct access in daily life. Gender is the means through which we "recognize" sex (Butler 1990, 1993). Consequently, gender is the cultural/discursive means of producing sex as natural—"a politically neutral surface *on which* culture acts" (emphasis in the original, Butler 1990, 7).

3. Even in feminist scholarship it is no longer unusual to see the terms sex and gender used interchangeably, to see the terms female and woman used interchangeably, or to see references to female and male as *genders*, rather than sexes. The lack of initial specificity between terms arises as well when male and female are used as adjectival forms of man and woman.

4. Harold Garfinkel developed and used breaching experiments as a means to disrupt, and thus reveal, assumptions that underpin daily interaction. For example, in the United States people commonly greet each other by saying, "How are you?" Breaching behavior might respond to this question with a detailed response about one's health. In this example what is being breached is the common knowledge that this question is a greeting and not an inquiry.

5. Later in this chapter I explore how discourse about race works through "gender" to produce whiteness as one of the attendant cultural meanings of "woman."

6. "Doing gender" consists of managing occasions so that "whatever the particulars, the outcome is seen and seeable in the context as gender-appropriate or, as the case may be, gender-inappropriate, that is accountable" (West and Zimmerman 1987, 135). To "'do' gender is not necessarily to live up to normative conceptions of femininity or masculinity; but to engage in behavior *at the risk of gender assessment*" (emphasis in the original, West and Zimmerman 1987, 136). In this sense, doing gender is a self-regulating process (West and Zimmerman 1987). By "doing gender" in interaction, we produce and maintain categorical differences that appear to be essential (West and Zimmerman 1987).

7. While sexed and gendered "natures" are far from natural, because gendered behavior is not optional—there is no alternative to gendered behavior since there is no human nature that stands apart—gender is an interactional accomplishment not a role (West and Zimmerman 1987).

8. While I refer to people I interviewed and to television characters by their first names, I refer to news anchors and reporters by their last names. This reflects my distinction of layers of representation among: real people, representations of real people, and those who are professional reporters intentionally portrayed as transparent bearers of news.

9. It may be worth noting that none of the people I interviewed were academics. Readers are referred to the demographic table in Appendix A for details.

10. I met Polard for the first time in this interview; the earlier portion of the interview did not include any discussion of sexuality. After more than two hours of conversation together, I take his comment to be a reflection of the "kind of person" he believed me to be, though I am uncertain if he read me as being queer.

11. Tamsin Wilton (1996) refers to this as the production of heterosexuality through "heteropolarity."

12. Because I am interested in the production of sexual "difference" in a heterosexual imaginary, I did not study shows that routinely feature queer people or issues, such as *Will & Grace*.

13. "For heterosexuality to achieve the status of the 'compulsory,' it must present itself as a practice governed by some internal necessity. The language and law that regulates the establishment of heterosexuality both as an identity and an institution, both a practice and a system, is the language and law of defense and protection: heterosexuality secures its self-identity and shores up its ontological boundaries by protecting itself from what it sees as the continual predatory encroachment of the contaminated other, homosexuality" (Fuss 1991, 2).

14. Berube (2001, 257) has argued that in its most narrow form, the gay rights project can be understood as an attempt by white men to regain the social status they had been raised to expect, as white men. The ability to look (and act) like those who are in power helps to sustain the minimal visible presence white gay men have achieved.

15. Lorraine's apparent acceptance of animal representations may be related to a world view that understands relationships among humans and other living beings quite differently than hegemonic U.S. culture. The reason for this particular emphasis is not clear.

16. In Chapter 5, I trace the development and evolution of characterizations of poor people and poverty in newspaper coverage from 1982 through 1996.

17. Ethnomethodology, also raised at the start, somewhat straddles this division, On one hand, it posits a subject constituted through language and interaction, yet it also holds a phenomenonologically-grounded analysis of agency and power. The undertheorization of agency and subjectivity in ethnomethodology, leads me to bracket it for this discussion.

Chapter 4

1. The Census Bureau does not publish data on the incomes of the top 1 percent; the Congressional Budget Office supplements Census data with IRS data to capture gains and losses among the top one percent of the population.
2. Consider for instance that while every major metropolitan newspaper has a daily business section, none has a comparable section for workers. Consequently, it seems that either the interests of workers and the interests of business are the same, or that the interests of workers are not relevant to national news.
3. "The insistence on a special relationship to the land as the basis for indigenous identity is not merely spiritual, an affirmation of an ecological sensibility, but also calls for a transformation of the spatial arrangements of colonialism or postcolonialism. Indigenism, in other words, challenges not just the relations between different ethnicities but the system of economic relations that provides the ultimate context for social and political relationships: capitalist or state socialist" (Dirlik 1996, 21).
4. My racial characterization of Brady, and of my interviewees in this chapter, comes from self-identifications on the interview exit form—unless otherwise noted.
5. In subsequent seasons, Judge Gray purchased the home from her mother, although the family configuration in the home remained the same.
6. An earlier version of the analysis in this section was published in *Cultural Studies<->Critical Methodologies,* 5(2):250–268.
7. Despite the pervasive presence of people unable to afford housing, homeless people live profoundly segregated lives. Typically for people who have housing, knowledge about homelessness and homeless people comes from news media, rather than from ongoing, personal relationships with people living on the street. As such, newspaper articles about homelessness offer a particularly rich analytic site for understanding the cultural production of homelessness.
8. For this line of thinking, I am indebted to my friendship and conversations with John Kelly.
9. See also, Garfinkel's (1967) work on sex status as a "managed achievement"; Kessler and McKenna's work on gender as an interactional accomplishment; Cahill's (1982; 1995) study on the acquisition and development of gender identity in toddlers and West and Zimmerman's (1987) "doing gender."
10. Frequently heralded as a bastion of radicalism, Santa Cruz is known for having a socialist mayor, one of the first openly gay mayors in the nation, and the audacity to turn the U.S. Navy away from its harbor on one Fourth of July in protest of the military. In 1994, when Santa Cruz passed some of the nation's most restrictive laws targeting the behavior of homeless people, the mayor was a well-noted war tax resister and a long-standing member of the local nonviolence community. If the passage of such laws might be dismissed as "politics as usual" in a more conservative milieu, this is definitely not the case in Santa Cruz.
11. I've borrowed this phrase from Battaglia (1995).

Chapter 5

1. Postmodern conceptions of identity struggle to escape an analytical conception of identity based on modernist notions of stable difference in which identities appear to be as much a process of exclusion as identification (Butler 1993; Grossberg 1996; Hall 1996, 1997a). This sense of identity requires a reification of processes, experiences, and consciousness into a "me," and establishes identity as a representational economy potentially at risk from entanglements with other "different" histories, experiences, and self-representations (Minh-ha 1997).

REFERENCES

Aanerud, Rebecca. 2003. Fictions of whitenes: Speaking the names of whiteness in U.S. literature. In *Displacing Whiteness*, ed. R. Frankenberg, 35–59. Durham, NC: Duke University Press.

Acker, Joan. 1973. Women and social stratification: A case of intellectual sexism. *American Journal of Sociology* 78:936–945.

Adams, Katherine. 2002. At the table with Arendt: Toward a self-interests practice of coalition discourse. *Hypatia* 17:1–33.

Ahmed, Sara. 1999. She'll wake up one of these days and find she's turned into a nigger: Passing and hybridity. In *Performativity and belonging*, ed. V. Bell, 87–116. London: Sage.

Alasutari, Pertti. 1995. *Researching Culture: Qualitative Method and Cultural Studies*. Thousand Oaks, CA: Sage.

Ablow, Keith Russell. 1991. Homeless, but not mentally ill. *Washington Post*, WH9, January 22.

Alexander, Jeffrey. 1990. Analytic debates: Understanding the relative autonomy of culture. In *Culture and Society: Contemporary Debate*, eds. J. Alexander and S. Seidman, 1–30. Cambridge: Cambridge University Press.

Almaguer, Tomás. 1974. Class, race and Chicano oppression. *Socialist Review* 5:71–100.

Almaguer, Tomas. 1994. *Racial Faultlines: The Historical Origins of White Supremacy in California*. Berkeley: University of California Press.

Althuser, Louis. 1971. *Lenin, Philosophy, and Other Essays*. London: New Left Books.

Alvarez, Fred. 1995. Floodwaters Sweep away inertia." *Los Angeles Times*, A1, A16, January 30.

Anzuldua, G. 1987. *Borderlands/La Frontera: The New Meztiza*. San Francisco: Spinsters/ Aunt Lute.

Appiah, Anthony. 1985. The uncompleted argument: Du Bois and the illusion of race. In *"Race," Writing, and Difference*, ed. J. Henry Louis Gates, 21–37. Chicago: University of Chicago.

Appiah, Anthony. 1992. *In My Father's House: Africa in the Philosophy of Culture*. New York: Oxford University Press.

Appiah, Kwame Anthony, and Amy Gutman. 1996. *Color Conscious: The Political Morality of Race*. Princeton, NJ: Princeton University Press.

Aptheker, Bettina. 1982. *Woman's Legacy: Essays on Race, Sex and Class in American History*. Amherst: University of Massachusetts Press.

———. 1989. *Tapestries of life: Women's Work, Women's Consciousness, and the Meaning of Daily Experience*. Amherst: University of Massachusetts Press.

Atkinson, Paul. 1988. Ethnomethodology: A critical review. *Annual Review of Sociology* (14):441–465.

Austin, J. L. 1962. *How to Do Things with Words*. Cambridge, MA: Harvard University Press.

Bailey, Eric. 1984. "Troll Busters" in Santa Cruz prey on the homeless. *Los Angeles Times*, 3, 36, October 26.

Bakhtin, Mikhail. 1981. *The Dialogic Imagination*. Austin: University of Texas.

———. 1986. *Speech Genres & Other Late Essays*. eds. C. Emerson and M. Holquist, trans. V. W. McGee. Austin: University of Texas Press.

Balibar, Etienne. 2002. *Politics and the Other Scene*. New York: Verso.

Balser, Barbara. 1985. Officials debate the number of mentally ill homeless. *New York Times*, B11, November 14.

Bannerji, Himani. 1995. *Thinking Through: Essays on Feminism, Marxism, and Anti-Racism*. Toronto: Women's Press.

Barbanel, Josh. 1987. Homeless woman sent to hospital under Koch plan is ordered free. *New York Times*, A1, B2, November 13.

Barker, Karlyn. 1986. Street woman: Long day's journey into night. *Washington Post*, A1, A11, February 16.

Basler, Barbara. 1985. Koch limits using welfare hotels. *New York Times*, A1, B13, December 17.

Bates, Steve. 1994. Alexandria asks hill for help on army base. *Washington Post*, C3, July 8.

Battaglia, Debbora. 1995. Problemitizing the self: A thematic introduction. In *Rhetorics of Self-Making*, ed. D. Battaglia, 1–15. Berkeley: University of California Press.

Bauman, Zygmunt. 1993. *Postmodern Ethics*. Oxford: Blackwell.

Belcher, J. (1983). Runaways. *Los Angeles Times*, v102, sec. II.

Bell, Vikki. 1999. *Performativity and Belonging*. Thousand Oaks, CA: Sage.

Bellah, Robert, Richard Madsen, William Sullivan, Ann Swidler, and Steven Tipton. 1991. *The Good Society*. New York: Alfred Knopf.

———. 1996. *Habits of the Heart: Individualism and Commitment in American Life*. Berkeley: University of California.

Benjamin, Jessica. 1995. Sameness and difference: Toward an "over-inclusive" theory of gender development. In *Psychoanalysis in Contexts: Paths Between Theory and Modern Culture*, eds. A. Elliott and S. Frosh, 106–122. New York: Routledge.

Berg, Bruce. 2007. *Qualitative Research Methods for the Social Sciences*. Boston: Pearson.

Berger, Peter, and Thomas Luckman. 1966. *The Social Construction of Reality: A Treatise in the Sociology of Knowledge*. Garden City, NY: Doubleday.

Berube, Allan. 2001. How gay stays white and what kind of white it stays. In *The Making and Unmaking of Whiteness*, eds. B. B. Rasmussen, E. Klinenberg, I. Nexica, and M. Wray, 234–265. Durham, NC: Duke University.

Bettie, Julie. 2003. *Women Without Class: Girls, Race, and Identity*. Berkeley: University of California Press.

Billig, Michael. 1997. From codes to utterances: *Cultural studies*, discourse and psychology. In *Cultural Studies in Question*, eds. by M. Ferguson and P. Golding, 205–226. Thousand Oaks, CA: Sage Publications.

———. 2003. Critical discourse analysis and the rhetoric of critique. *In Critical Discourse Analsyis: Theory and Interdisciplinarity*, eds. G. Weiss and R. Wodak, 35–46. New York: Palgrave MacMillan.

Billig, Michael, Susan Condor, Derek Edwards, Mike Gane, David Middleton, and Alan Radley. 1998. Ideological Dilemmas: *A Social Psychology of Everyday Thinking*. Newbury Park, CA: Sage.

Bjelic, Dusan, and Michael Lynch. 1992. The work of a (scientific) demonstration: Respecifying Newton's and Goethe's theories of prismatic color. In *Text in Context: Contributions to Ethnomethodology*, eds. G. Watson and R. Seiler, 52–78. Newbury Park, CA: Sage.

Blau, Joel. 1992. *The Visible Poor: Homelessness in the United States*. New York: Oxford University Press.

Blauner, Bob. 1989. *Black Lives, White Lives: Three Decades of Race Relations in America*. Berkeley: University of California Press.

Blee, Kathleen M. 1991. *Women of the Klan: Racism and Gender in the 1920s*. Berkeley: University of California Press.

Blimes, Jack. 1992. Mishearings. In *Text in Context: Contributions to Ethnomethodology*, eds. G. Watson and R. Seiler, 79–98. Newbury Park, CA: Sage Publications.

Bonacich, Edna. 1972. A Theory of Ethnic Antagonism: The split labor market. *American Sociology Review* 37:547–559.

Bonilla-Silva, Eduardo, and Ashley W. Doane. 2003. *White Out: The Continuing Significance of Racism*. New York: Routledge.

Bordo, Susan. 1993. *Unbearable Weight: Feminism, Western Culture and the Body*. Berkeley: University of California Press.

———. 1999. *Twilight Zones: The Hidden Life of Cultural Images from Plato to O.J.* Berkeley: University of California Press.

Bornstien, Kate. 1994. *Gender Outlaw: On Men, Women and the Rest of Us*. New York: Vintage Books.

Bourdieu, Pierre. 1996. *Distinction: A Social Critique of the Judgment of Taste*. Translated by R. Nice. Cambridge, MA: Harvard University Press.

Brisbane, Arthur. 1985. Homeless caught in conflict. *Washington Post*, A1, A10.

Broder, David. 1991. Mayors discern growth in mentally ill homeless. *Washington Post*, A2, November 9.

Brownmiller, Susan. 1976. *Against Our Will: Men, Women and Rape*. New York: Simon and Schuster.

Bruegel, Irene. 1979. Women as a reserve army of labour: A note on recent British experience. *Feminist Review* 3:12–23.

Bullough, Vern L. 2001. Transgenderism and the concept of gender. *International Journal of Transgenderism*, 5, No. 1.

Bunch, Charlotte. 1987. *Passionate Politics: Feminist Theory in Action, Essays 1968–1986*. New York: St. Martin's.

Butler, Judith. 1990. *Gender Trouble: Feminism and the Subversion of Identity*. New York: Routledge.

———. 1991. *Imitation and Gender Insubordination. In Inside/Out: Lesbian Theories, Gay Theories*, ed. D. Fuss, 13–31. New York: Routledge.

———. 1993. *Bodies that Matter*. London: Routledge.

———. 1995. Contingent foundations: Feminism and the question of "postmodernism." In *Feminist Contentions: A Philosophical Exchange*, eds. S. Benhabib, J. Butler, D. Cornell, and N. Fraser, 35–57. New York: Routledge.

———. 1997a. *Excitable Speech: A Politics of the Performative*. New York: Routledge.

———. 1997b. Gender is burning: Questions of appropriation and subversion. In *Dangerous Liaisons: Gender, Nation and Postcolonial Perspectives*, eds. A. McClintock, A. Mufti, and E. Shohat, 381–395. Minneapolis: University of Minnesota.

———. 1997c. *The Psychic Life of Power: Theories in Subjection*. Stanford, CA: Stanford University Press.

———. 1999. On speech, race, and melancholia. In *Performativity and Belonging*, ed. V. Bell, 163–173. Thousand Oaks, CA: Sage.

Cahill, Spencer Ernest. 1982. *Becoming Boys and Girls*. PhD thesis, University of California, Santa Barbara.

———. 1995. Language practices and self-definition. In *Inside Social Life: Readings on Sociological Psychology and Microsociology*, ed. S. E. Cahill, 26–31. Los Angeles: Roxbury Publishing Company.

Campbell, Richard and Jimmie Reeves. 1999. Covering the homeless: The Joyce Brown story. In *Reading the Homeless: The Media's Image of Homeless Culture*, ed. E. Min, 23–44. Westport, CT: Praeger.

Carby, Hazel V. 1987. *Reconstructing Womanhood: The Emergence of the Afro-American Woman Novelist*. New York: Oxford University Press.

———. 1997. White woman listen! Black feminism and the boundaries of sisterhood. In *Materialist Feminism: A Reader in Class, Difference, and Women's Lives*, eds. R. Hennessy and C. Ingraham, 110–128. New York: Routledge.

Casetti, Franceso. 1999. *Theories of Cinema, 1945–1995*. Trans. F. Chiostri, E. Gard Bartolini-Salimbeni, and T. Kelso. Austin: University of Texas Press.

Center on Budget and Policy Priorities. 2006. Poverty increases and median income declines for second consecutive year. Center on Budget and Policy Priorities 2003 [cited Fall 2005]. Available from http://www.cbpp.org/9-26-03pov.htm.

Chabram-Dernersesian, Angie. 1997. On the social construction of whiteness within selected Chicana/o discourses. In *Displacing Whiteness*, ed. R. Frankenberg, 107–164. Durham, NC: Duke University Press.

Childs, John Brown. 1998. From the politics of conversion to the ethics of respect: Learning from native American philosophies. *Social Justice* 25:143–169.

Clarke, Adele E. 2005. *Situational Analysis: Grounded Theory After the Postmodern Turn*. Thousand Oaks, CA: Sage Publications.

Clough, Patricia. 2000. *Autoaffection*. Minneapolis: University of Minnesota Press.

Cohen, Jerry. 1984. A few weeks in paradise for urban nomads. *Los Angeles Times*, 1.

Collins, Patricia Hill. 1993. Black feminist thought in the matrix of domination. In *Social Theory: The Multicultural & Classical Readings*, ed. C. Lemert, 553–563. San Francisco: Westview Press.

Collins, Scott. 1995. Dispute over homeless heats up with Goldberg's support of center. *Los Angeles Times*, B4, September 6.

Cook, Pam, and Claire Johnston. 1988. The place of woman in the cinema of Raoul Walsh. In *Feminism and Film Theory*, ed. C. Penley, 25–35. New York: Routledge.

Cowie, Elizabeth. 1988. The popular film as a progressive text—a discussion of coma—part 1. In *Feminism and Film Theory*, ed. C. Penley, 104–140. New York: Routledge.

———. 1999. The spectacle of actuality. In *Collecting Visible Evidence*, vol. 6, eds. J. M. Gaines and M. Renov, 19–45. Minneapolis: University of Minnesota Press.

Cox, Oliver Cromwell. 1959. *Caste, Class & Race: A Study in Social Dynamics*. New York: Monthly Review Press.

Crenshaw, Kimberle. 1991. Mapping the margins: Intersectionality, identity politics and violence against women of color. *Stanford Law Review* 43:1241–1299.

———. 1992. Whose story is it anyway? Feminist and anti-racist appropriations of Anita Hill. In *Race-ing Justice, En-Gendering Power: Essays on Anita Hill*, Clarence Thomas, and the construction of social reality, ed. T. Morrison, 402–441. New York: Pantheon.

Crenshaw, Kimberle, Neil Gotanda, Garry Peller, and Kendall Thomas. 1995. *Critical Race Theory: The Key Writings that Formed the Movement*. New York: New York Press.

Dahrendorf, Ralf. 1959. *Class and Class Conflict in Industrial Society*, vol. Stanford, CA: Stanford University Press.

———. 1967. *Conflict After Class: New Perspectives on the Theory of Social and Political Conflict*. Essex: The University of Essex.

———. 1979. *Life Chances: Approaches to Social and Political Theory*. London: Weidenfield and Nocolson.

Daly, Mary. 1978. *Gyn/ecology: The Meta-Ethics of Radical Feminism*. Boston: Beacon Press.

Daunt, Tina. 1994. Council oks plan for homeless center. *Los Angeles Times*, B1, November 9.

Davis, Angela Y. 1983. *Women, Race & Class*. New York: Vintage Books.

de Certeau, Michel. 1984. *The Practice of Everyday Life*. Trans. S. Rendall. Berkeley: University of California Press.

Dei, George J. Sefa, Leeno Luke Karumanchery, and Nisha Karumanchery-Luik. 2004. *Playing the Race Card: Exposing White Power and Privilege*. New York: Peter Lang.

Delgado, Richard. 1982. Words that wound: A tort action for racial insults, epithets and name-calling. *Harvard Civil Rights Civil Liberties Law Review* 17:133–181.

———. 1995. *Critical Race Theory: The Cutting Edge*. Philadelphia: Temple University Press.

———. 1998. Are hate speech rules constitutional heresy? A reply to Steven Gey. *University of Pennsylvania Law Review*:146–182, March.

Delgado-P, Guillermo. 1994. Ethnic politics and the popular movements. In *Latin American Faces the 21st Century*, ed. S. A. E. M. Jonas, 1–12. London: Westview.

Denny, Dallas. 1998. *Current Concepts in Transgender Identity*. New York: Garland.

Denzin, Norman. 1989. *The Research Act: A Theoretical Introduction to Sociological Methods* (3rd ed.). Englewood Cliffs, NJ: Prentice-Hall

———. 1990. Harold and Agnes: A feminist narrative undoing. *Sociological Theory* 8:198–216.

———. 1991. Back to Harold and Agnes. *Sociological Theory* 9:280–285.

———. 1992. *Symbolic Interactionism and Cultural Studies*. Cambridge: Blackwell.

———. 2001. Symbolic interactionism, poststructuralism, and the racial subject. *Symbolic Interaction* 24:243–249.

———. 2002. The cinematic society and the reflexive interview." In *Handbook of Interview Research: Context and Method*, eds. J. Gubrium and J. Holstein, 833–848. Thousand Oaks, CA: Sage Publications.

Denzin, Norman, and Yvonne Lincoln. 2003. Introduction: The discipline and practice of qualitative research. In *Collecting and Interpreting Qualitative Materials*, eds. N. Denzin and Y. Lincoln, 1–45. Thousand Oaks, CA: Sage Publications.

Derrida, Jacques. 1972a. *Limited Inc*. Evanston, IL: Northwestern University Press.

———. 1972b. *Positions*. Chicago: University of Chicago Press.

———. 1976. *On Gramatology*. Baltimore: Johns Hopkins University Press.

———. 1982. *Margins of Philosophy*. Trans. A. Bass. Chicago: University of Chicago.

Dill, Bonnie Thornton. 1992. Our mother's grief: Racial ethnic women and the maintenance of families. *In Race, Class, and Gender: An Anthology*, eds. M. Andersen and P. H. Collins, 215–238. Belmont, CA: Wadsworth.

Dirlik, Arif. 1996. The past as legacy and project: Postcolonial criticism in the perspective of indigenous historicism. *American Indian Culture and Research Journal* 20:1–31.

Dolan, Maura. 1994. Narrow ruling is expected on homeless law. *Los Angeles Times*, A3, A37.

Douglas, Jack. 1970. *Understanding Everyday Life: Toward the Reconstruction of Social Knowledge*. Chicago: Aldine.

Du Bois, W.E.B. 1995a. *Black Reconstruction in America, 1860–1880*. New York: Touchstone

du Gay, Paul. 1996. *Consumption and Identity at Work*. London: Sage.

du Toit, Andries. 2005. Poverty measurement blues: Some reflections on the space for understanding "chronic" and "structural" poverty in South Africa. In *First International Congress on Qualitative Inquiry*, ed. N. Denzin, Paper ID I-295-du Toit. Urbana-Champaign: University of Illinois at Urbana-Champaign.

Dunn, Robert. 1997. Self, identity and difference: Mead and the poststructuralists. *Sociological Quarterly* 38:687–705.

Dworkin, Andrea. 1974. *Woman Hating*. New York: E.P. Dutton.

Eco, Umberto. 1998. *Serendipity: Language and Lunacy*. New York: Columbia University Press.

Eisenstein, Zillah. 1990. Constructing a theory of capitalist patriarchy and socialist feminism. In *Women, Class and the Feminist Imagination: A Socialist-Feminist Reader*, eds. K. Hansen and I. Philipson, 114–145. Philadelphia: Temple University Press.

Engel, Margaret. 1983. Kicked out: As evictions strike the middle class, the list of homeless grows longer. *Washington Post*, A1, A6, February 23.

Engels, Frederick. 1978. The origin of the family, private property, and the state. In *The Marx-Engels Reader*, ed. R. C. Tucker, 734–759. New York: W.W. Norton.

Essed, Philomena. 1991. *Understanding Everyday Racism: An Interdisciplinary Theory*. Newbury Park, CA: Sage Publications.

Eze, Emmanuel Chukwudi. 1997. *Postcolonial African Philosophy*. Cambridge, MA: Blackwell.

Fairclough, Norman. 1992. *Discourse and Social Change*. New York: Polity Press.

———. 1995. *Critical Discourse Analysis: The Critical Study of Language*. Harlow: Longman.

Fairclough, Norman, and Ruth Wodak. 1997. Critical discourse analysis. In *Discourse as Social Interaction*, ed. T. A. Van Dijik, 258–284. Thousand Oaks, CA: Sage.

Fenstermaker, Sarah, Candace West, and Don Zimmerman. 1991. Gender inequality: New conceptual terrain. In *Gender Family and Economy: The Triple Overlap*, ed.y R. L. Blumberg, 289–307. Newbury Park, CA: Sage.

Ferree, Myra Marx, and Elaine Hall. 1996. Rethinking stratification from a feminist perspective: Gender, race, and class in mainstream textbooks. *American Sociological Review* 61:929–950.

Ferrell, David, and Sonia Nazario. 1993. Residents more wary of squatters in the hillsides. *Los Angeles Times*, A1, A9, October 30.

Fields, Barbara Jeanne. 1983. The nineteenth century south: History and theory. *Plantation Society in the Americas* 2:7–27.

———. 1990. Slavery, race and ideology in the United States of America. *New Left Review* May/June:95–118.

Fiske, John. 1999. For cultural interpretation: A study of the culture of homelessness. In *Reading the Homeless: The Media's Image of Homeless Culture*, ed. E. Min, 1–22. Westport, CT: Praeger.

Foley, Neil. 1997. Becoming Hispanic: Mexican Americans and the fautian pact with whiteness. In *New Directions in Mexican American Studies*, ed. R. Flores, 53–70. Austin: University of Texas.

Foner, Eric. 1988. *Reconstruction: America's Unfinished Revolution*: 1863–1877. New York: Harper & Row.

———. 1990. *A Short History of Reconstruction, 1863–1877*. New York: Harper & Row.

Foner, Eric, and Olivia Mahoney. 1995. *America's Reconstruction: People and Politics After the Civil War*. New York: HarperPerennial.

Foucault, Michel. 1970. *The Order of Things: An Archaeology of the Human Sciences*. New York: Vintage Books.

———. 1972. *The Archeology of Knowledge*. Trans. A. M. S. Smith. New York: Pantheon Books.

———. 1977. *Discipline and Punish: The Birth of the Prison*. Trans. A. Sheridan. New York: Vintage Books.

———. 1978. *The History of Sexuality, Vol. 1: An Introduction*. Trans. R. Hurley. New York: Vintage Books.

———. 1980. *Power/Knowledge: Selected Interviews and Other Writings 1972–1977.* ed. C. Gordon, trans. C. Gordon, L. Marsahll, J. Mepham, and K. Soper. New York: Pantheon Books.

———. 1994. *Ethics, Subjectivity and Truth*, Vol. 1. Ed. P. Rabinow, trans. R. Hurley and others. New York: The New Press.

Frankenberg, Ruth. 1993. *The Social Construction of Whiteness: White Women, Race Matters.* Minneapolis: University of Minnesota Press.

———. 1997a. *Displacing Whiteness: Essays in Social and Cultural Criticism.* Durham, NC: Duke University Press.

———. 1997b. Introduction: Local whiteness, localizing whiteness. In *Displacing Whiteness*, ed. R. Frankenberg, 1–34. Durham, NC: Duke University Press.

Fraser, Nancy, and Linda Nicholson. 1996. Social criticism without philosophy: An encounter between feminism and postmodernism. In *Feminist Literary Theory*, ed. M. Eagleton, 19–38. Oxford: Blackwell.

Fregoso, Rosa Linda, and Angie Chabram. 1994. Chicana/o cultural representations: Reframing alternative critical discourses. *Cultural Studies* 4:203–213.

Frye, Marilyn. 1983. *The Politics of Reality: Essays in Feminist Theory.* New York: Crossings Press.

Fuss, Diana. 1989. *Essentially Speaking.* New York: Routledge.

———. 1991. *Inside/Out.* New York: Routledge.

Gaines, Jane M. 1999. Introduction: The real returns. In *Collecting Visible Evidence*, vol. 6, eds. J. M. Gaines and M. Renov, 1–18. Minneapolis: University of Minnesota Press.

Gamson, Joshua. 1998. *Freaks Talk Back.* Chicago: University of Chicago.

Garber, Marjorie. 1992. *Vested Interests.* New York: Routledge.

Garfinkel, Harold. 1967. *Studies in Ethnomethodology.* Cambridge: Polity Press.

Garfinkel, Harold, and Harvey Sacks. 1970. On formal structure and practical actions. In *Theoretical Sociology: Perspectives and Development*, eds. J. McKinney and E. Tiraykian, 338–366. New York: Appleton-Century-Crofts.

Garnsey, Elizabeth. 1982. Women's work and theories of class stratification. In *Classes, Power, and Conflict: Classical and Contemporary Debates*, eds. A. Giddens and D. Held, 425–445. Berkeley: University of California.

Geertz, Clifford. 1983. *Local Knowledge: Further Essays in Interpretative Anthropology.* New York: Basic Books.

Gibson-Graham, J. K. 1999. *The End of Capitalism (As We Knew It).* New York: Blackwell.

Gibson-Graham, J. K., Stephen Resnick, and Richard Wolff. 2001. *Re/Pesenting Class: Essays in Postmodern Marxism.* Durham, NC: Duke University Press.

Gilbert, G. Nigel, and Michael Mulkay. 1984. *Opening Pandora's Box: A Sociological Analysis of Scientists' Discourse.* Cambridge: Cambridge University Press

Gilroy, Paul. 1992. *Cultural studies* and ethnic absolutism. In *Cultural Studies*, ed. L. Grossberg, 187–197. New York: Routledge.

———. 1993. *The Black Atlantic: Modernity and Double-Consciousness.* Cambridge, MA: Harvard University Press.

———. 2000. *Against Race: Imagining Political Culture Beyond the Color Line.* Cambridge, MA: Harvard University Press.

Glenn, Evelyn Nakano. 1985. Racial ethnic women's labor: The intersection of race, gender and class oppression. *Review of Radical Political Economics* 17:86–108.

———. 2002. *Unequal Freedom.* Cambridge, MA: Harvard University Press.

Glionna, John. 1993. Rhyme and reason: Poetry helps homeless man cope with life on the streets. *Los Angeles Times*, B1, May 21.

Goldberg, David Theo. 1993. *Racist Culture: Philosophy and the Politics of Meaning.* Cambridge, MA: Blackwell.

Goodwin, Michael. 1983. Rabbi rebutted by Koch in dispute on homeless. *New York Times*, 12, February 5.

Gordon, Avery. 1997. *Ghostly Matters: Haunting and the Sociological Imagination*. Minneapolis: University of Minnesota Press.

Gordon, David, Richard Edwards, and Michael Reich. 1982. *Segmented Work, Divided Workers: The Historical Transformation of Labor in the United States*. Cambridge: Cambridge University Press.

Gramsci, Antonio. 1971. *Selections from the Prison Notebooks of Antonio Gramsci*. Trans. Quintin Hoare and Geoffrey Nowel Smith. New York: International.

Gray, Herman. 1995a. Black masculinity and visual culture. *Callaloo* 18:401–405.

——— 1995b. *Watching Race: Television and the Struggle for "Blackness."* Minneapolis: University of Minnesota.

Grossberg, Lawrence. 1996. Identity and cultural studies: Is that all there is? In *Questions of Cultural Identity*, eds. S. Hall and P. du Gay, 87–107. Thousand Oaks, CA: Sage.

Grosz, Elizabeth. 1990. *Jacques Lacan: A Feminist Introduction*. London: Routledge.

Gubrium, Jaber, and James Holstein. 1997. *The New Language of Qualitative Method*. New York: Oxford University Press.

Guillaumin, Colette. 1995. *Racism, Sexism, Power, and Ideology*. New York: Routledge.

Guillermoprieto, Alma. 1984. Street people savor decision allowing them right to vote. *Washington Post*, C1, C7.

Guinier, Lani, and Gerald Torres. 2002. *The Miner's Canary: Enlisting Race, Resisting Power, Transforming Democracy*. Cambridge, MA: Harvard University Press.

Gusfield, Joseph. 1975. Categories of ownership and responsibility in social issues: Alcohol abuse and automobile use. *Journal of Drug Issues* 5:528–303.

Habermas, Jürgen. 1993. *Justification and Application: Remarks on Discourse Ethics*. Trans. C. P. Cronin. Cambridge, MA: MIT Press.

Hak, Tony. 1992. Psychiatric records as transformations of other texts. In *Text in Context: Contributions to Ethnomethodology*, eds. G. Watson and R. Seiler, 138–155. Newbury Park, CA: Sage.

Hall, Stuart. 1975. *Television as a Medium and its Relation to Culture*. Birmingham: Center for Contemporary *Cultural Studies*.

———. 1980. Cultural studies and the centre: Some problematics and problems. In *Culture, Media, Language*, eds. S. Baron, M. Denning, S. Hall, D. Hobson, and P. Willis, 15–47. London: Hutchinson.

———. 1986. Introduction. In *Politics and Ideology*, eds. J. Donald and S. Hall, ixxx. Oxford: Open University Press.

———. 1991. Old and New Identities: Old and new ethnicities. In *Culture, Globalization and The World System: Contemporary conditions for the representation of identity*, ed. A. King. Binghamton: State University of New York.

———. 1993. What is "black" in black popular culture? (Rethinking race). *Social Justice* 20:104–115.

———. 1996. Introduction: Who Needs Identity? In *Questions of Cultural Identity*, eds. S. Hall and P. du Gay, 1–17. London: Sage.

———. 1997a. Cultural identity and diaspora. In *Identity and Difference: Culture, Media and Identities*, ed. K. Woodward, 51–59. London: Sage Publications in association with The Open University.

———. 1997b. *Representation & the Media*, ed. S. Jhally. Northampton: Media Education Foundation.

———. 1997c. *Representation: Cultural and Signifying Practices*. Thousand Oaks, CA: Sage.

———. 1997d. The spectacle of the "Other." In *Representation: Cultural Representations and Signifying Practices*, ed. S. Hall, 223–290. Thousand Oaks, CA: Sage.

————. 1997e. The work of representation. In *Representation: Cultural Representations and Signifying Practices*, ed. S. Hall, 1–74. Thousand Oaks, CA: Sage.

Handel, Warren. 1982. *Ethnomethodology: How People Make Sense*. Englewood Cliffs, NJ: Prentice-Hall, Inc.

Haraway, Donna. 1991. *Simians, Cyborgs, and Women: The Reinvention of Nature*. New York: Routledge.

Harding, Sandra. 1991. *Whose Science? Whose Knowledge?* Ithaca, NY: Cornell University Press.

Hartmann, Heidi. 1982. *Capitalism, Patriarchy, and Job Segregation by Sex*. In Classes, power, and conflict: Classical and contemporary debates, eds. A. Giddens and D. Held, 446–469. Berkeley: University of California Press.

Hartsock, Nancy. 1987. The feminist standpoint: Developing the ground for a specific feminist historical materialism. In *Feminism and Methodology*, ed. S. Harding, 159–166. Bloomington: Indiana University Press.

Heap, James. 1992. Normative order in collaborative computer editing. In *Text in Context: Contributions to Ethnomethodology*, eds. G. Watson and R. Seiler, 123–137. Newbury Park, CA: Sage.

Hennessy, Rosemary. 1993. *Materialist Feminism and the Politics of Discourse*. New York: Routledge.

————. 2000. *Profit and Pleasure: Sexual Identities in Late Capitalism*. New York: Routledge.

Henry, Neil. 1984. Where the homeless get a second chance. *Washington Post*, A1, A16, October 7.

Hepburn, Alexa. 1997. Teachers and secondary school bullying: A postmodern analysis. *Discourse and Society* 8:27–48.

Heritage, John. 1984. *Garfinkle and Ethnomethodology*. Cambridge: Polity Press.

Heritage, John, and J. Maxwell Atkinson. 1992. Introduction. In *Structures of Social Action: Studies in Conversation Analysis*, eds. J. Heritage and J. M. Atkinson, 1–15. Cambridge: Cambridge University Press.

Herman, Robin. 1982. New York trying to add shelters for its homeless. *New York Times*, B3, July 26.

Hester, Stephen. 1992. Recognizing references to deviance in referral talk. In *Text in Context: Contributions to Ethnomethodology*, eds. G. Watson and R. Seiler, 156–174. Newbury Park, CA: Sage.

Hilbert, Richard. 1991. Norman and Sigmund: Comment on Denzin's "Harold and Agnes." *Sociological Theory* 9:264–268.

————. 1992. *The Classical Roots of Ethnomethodology: Durkheim, Weber, and Garfinkel*. Chapel Hill: University of North Carolina Press

Hill-Holtzman, Nancy. 1992. The battle for Santa Monica's parks. *Los Angeles Times*, B1, January 18.

Holstein, James, and Jaber Gubrium. 2000. *The Self We Live By: Narrative Identity in a Postmodern World*. Oxford: Oxford University Press

————. 2005. Interpretive practice and social action. In *The Sage Handbook of Qualitative Research*, eds. N. Denzin and Y. Lincoln, 483–505. Thousand Oaks, CA: Sage.

Holstein, James, and Gale Miller. 1993. Social constructionism and social problems work. In *Reconsidering Social Constructionism*, eds. J. Holstein and G. Miller, 151–172. New York: Aldine de Gruyter.

hooks, bell. 1992. Representing whiteness in the black imagination. In *Cultural Studies*, eds. L. Grossberg, C. Nelson, and A. Treichler, 338–346. New York: Routledge.

Horkheimer, Max. 1995. *Between Philosophy and Social Science*. Trans. M. K. Frederick Hunter, and John Torpey. Cambridge, MA: MIT Press. (Orig. pub. 1933.)

Horkheimer, Max, and Theodor Adorno. 1996. *Dialectic of Enlightenment*. Trans. J. Cumming. New York: Continuum.

Hubler, Shawn. 1992. Stranger lends a hand to those on life's off-ramp. *Los Angeles Times*, A1, A26, June 13.

Hull, Gloria T., Patricia Bell Scott, and Barbara Smith. 1982. *All the Women are White, all the Blacks are Men, but Some of Us are Brave*. Old Westbury, NY: The Feminist Press.

Human Rights Campaign. Laws in your state 2005 [cited 2005]. Available from http://hrc.org/.

Husserl, Edmund. 1962. *Ideas: General Introduction to Pure Phenomenology*. Trans. W. R. B. Gibson. New York: Collier.

Ifill, Gwen. 1990. Some cities reviving SRO hotels in effort against homelessness. *Washington Post*, A3, April 21.

Ignatiev, Noel. 1995. *How the Irish Became White*. New York: Routledge.

Ingraham, Chrys. 1997. The heterosexual imaginary. In *Materialist Feminism: A Reader in Class, Difference, and Women's Lives*, eds. R. Hennessy and C. Ingraham, 275–290. New York: Routledge.

Jackson, Alecia Youngblood. 2004. Performativity identified. *Qualitative Inquiry* 10:673–690.

Jackson, Stevi. 1998. Theorising gender and sexuality. In *Contemporary Feminist Theories*, eds. S. Jackson and J. Jones, 131–143. Edinburgh: Edinburgh University Press.

Jackson, Stevi and Jackie Jones. 1998. Thinking for ourselves: An introduction. In *Contemporary Feminist Theories*, eds. S. Jackson and J. Jones, 1–11. Edinburgh: Edinburgh University Press.

Jenness, Valerie. 1995. Hate crimes in the United States: The transformation of injured persons into victims and the extension of victim status to multiple constituencies. In *Images of Issues: Typifying Contemporary Social Problems*, ed. J. Best, 213–238. New York: Aldine de Gruyter.

Johnson, E. Patrick. 2003. *Appropriating Blackness: Performance and the Politics of Authenticity*. Durham, NC: Duke University Press.

Jones, Jacqueline. 1985. *Labor of Love, Labor of Sorrow: Black Women, Work and the Family from Slavery to the Present*. New York: Basic Books.

Kelley, Robin D. G. 1994. *Race Rebels: Culture, Politics, and the Black Working Class*. New York: The Free Press.

Kerr, Peter. 1985a. Homelessness isn't skipping a generation on city streets. *New York Times*, E7, November 3.

———. 1985b. Suburbs struggle with rise in the homeless. *New York Times*, 1, 44, December 22.

———. 1986. Why so many are priced out of the market? *New York Times*, E5, March 1.

Kessler, Suzanne. 2001. Who put the "Trans" in transgender? Gender theory and everyday life. vol. 5,1. *International Journal of Transgenderism*. http://symposion/com/ijt/gilbert/kessler.htm. Accessed February 20, 2006.

Kessler, Suzanne, and Wendy McKenna. 1978. *Gender: An Ethnomethodological Approach*. New York: Wiley.

Kincheloe, Joe, and Peter McLaren. 1998. Rethinking critical theory and qualitative research. In *The Landscape of Qualitative Research*, eds. N. Denzin and Y. S. Lincoln, 260–299. Thousand Oaks, CA: Sage.

Krikorian, Greg. 1996. Judge assails Garcetti for treating drug charge as "3rd strike" case. In *Los Angeles Times*, B3, March 8.

Kuhn, Thomas. 1970. *The Structure of Scientific Revolutions*. Chicago: University of Chicago Press.

Lacey, Marc. 1995. A long walk from skid wow to the white house. *Los Angeles Times*, 3.

Laclau, Ernesto, and Chantal Mouffe. 1985. *Hegemony & Socialist Strategy: Towards a Radical Democratic Politics*. New York: Verso.

LaDuke, Winona. 1995. The indigenous women's network our future, our responsibility, United Nations Fourth World Conference on Women, Bejing, China. http://radical.org/co-globalize/winonaladuke/beiging95.html. Accessed June 19, 1998.

Lambda. 2005. Lambda legal 2005. Available from http://www.lambdalegal.org/cgi-bin/iowa/index.html.

Lamont, Michele. 1992. *Money, Morals, & Manners*. Chicago: University of Chicago Press.

Latour, Bruno. 1993. *We Have Never Been Modern*. Cambridge, MA: Harvard University Press.

Leder, Laura, and Richard Delgado. 1995. *The Price We Pay: The Case Against Racist Speech, Hate Propaganda and Pronography*. New York: Hill and Wang.

Lefebvre, Henri. 1947. *Critique of Everyday Life*, vol. 1. Trans. J. Moore. New York: Verso.

Lembo, Ron. 2000. *Thinking through Television*. Cambridge: Cambridge University Press.

Lemert, Charles. 1979. De-centered analysis: Ethnomethodology and structuralism. *Theory and Society* 7:289–306.

Levine, Bettuane. 1994. A place to call home. *Los Angeles Times*, E1, E5, December 28.

Lewin, Tamar. 1987. Nation's homeless veterans battle a new foe: Defeatism. *New York Times*, A1, A10, December 30.

Lipsitz, George. 1998. *The Possessive Investment in Whiteness*. Philadelphia: Temple University Press.

Loeb, Vernon. 1995. For homeless, no shelter from the cutbacks; D.C.'s budget troubles threaten model U.S. effort. *Washington Post*. B1, B6, November 27.

Long, Elizabeth. 1997. Introduction. In *From Sociology to Cultural Studies*, ed. E. Long, 1–32. Malden, MA: Blackwell.

Lopez, Ian Haney. 1996. *White by Law: The Legal Construction of Race*. New York: New York University Press.

Lorch, Donatella. 1992. Hotel in Queens is focus of shift on the homeless. *New York Times*, A1, B2, February 7.

Lowe, Lisa. 1996. *Immigrant Acts*. Durham, NC: Duke University Press.

Lubiano, Wahneema. 1992. Black ladies, welfare queens, and state minstrels: Ideological war by narrative means. In *Race-ing Justice, En-Gendering Power: Essays on Anita Hill, Clarence Thomas, and the Construction of Social Reality*, ed. T. Morrison, 321–361. New York: Pantheon Books.

———. 1997a. *The House that Race Built*. New York: Vintage Books.

———. 1997b. Introduction. In *The House that Race Built*, ed. W. Lubiano, vii–ix. New York: Vintage Books.

Lynch, Michael, and David Bogen. 1994. Harvey Sack's primitive natural science. *Theory, Culture & Society* 11:65–104.

Mack, Arien. 1993. Home: *A Place in the World*. New York: New York University Press.

Maines, David R. 1977. Social organization and social structure in symbolic interactionist thought. *Annual Review of Sociology* 3:235–259.

Markle, Gerald, and Ronald Troyer. 1979. Smoke gets in your eyes: Cigarette smoking as deviant behavior. *Social Problems* 26:611–625.

Martinot, Steve. 2003. *The Rule of Racialization: Class, Identity, Governance*. Philadelphia: Temple University Press.

Marx, Karl. 1978. *The Marx-Engels Reader*, ed. R. C. Tucker. New York: W.W. Norton. (originally published in 1872).

———. 1990 (1875). *Capital*, vol. 1. Trans. B. Fowkes. New York: Penguin Books.

Mathews, Jay. 1987. Homeless shelter officials differ on problem's scope, nature. *Washington Post*. A4, A5.

Matsuda, Mari J. 1989. Public response to racist speech: Considering the victim's story. *Michigan Law Review* 87:2320–2381.

Matsuda, Mari, Charles Lawrence, Richard Delgado, and Kimberle Crenshaw. 1993. In *Words that Wound: Critical Race Theory, Assaultive Speech, and the First Amendment*, ed. R. Gordon and M. Radin, 1–16. Boulder, CO: Westview Press.

May, Clifford. 1986. The homeless: An urban condition spreads to suburbs. *New York Times*, B1, December 31.

Maynard, Douglas. 1991. Goffman, Garfinkel, and games. *Sociological Theory* 9:277–279.

Maynard, Douglas, and Steven Clayman. 1991. The diversity of ethnomethodology. *Annual Review of Sociology* 17:385–418.

McCarthy, Coleman. 1982. The shocking truth about the homeless. *Washington Post*, H4, December 26.

McClintock, Anne. 1995. *Imperial Leather: Race, Gender, and Sexuality in the Imperial Contest*. London: Routledge.

McHoul, Alec, and Wendy Grace. 1993. *A Foucault Primer: Discourse, Power and the Subject*. New York: New York University Press.

McLaughlin, K. 2002. Noisy protest against controls. In *San Jose Mercury News*, B1, B7.

McMillan, Penelope. 1990. Weingart center's head applies vorporate cures to skid row ills. *Los Angeles Times*, B1, B4, March 10.

Memmi, Albert. 2000. *Racism*. Trans. S. Martinot. Minneapolis: University of Minnesota Press.

Merleau-Ponty, Maurice. 1964. *Sense and Nonsense*. Trans. H. L. Dreyfus and P. A. Dreyfus. Evanston, IL: Northwestern University.

Mies, Maria. 1986. *Patriarchy and Accumulation on a World Scale: Women in the International Division of Labor*. London Zed Books.

Miles, Harvey. 1984. Food, clothing, shelter urged for mentally ill. *Los Angeles Times*, 5.

Miller, Gale, and Kathryn Fox. 2004. Building bridges: The possibility of analytic dialogue between ethnography, conversation analysis, and Foucault. In *Qualitative Research*, ed. D. Silverman, 33–55. Thousand Oaks, CA: Sage.

Miller, Leslie. 1990. Violent families and the rhetoric of harmony. *British Journal of Sociology* 41:263–288.

———. 1993. Claims-making from the underside: Marginalization and social problems analysis. In *Reconsidering Social Constructionism*, eds. J. Holstein and G. Miller, 349–376. New York: Aldine de Gruyter.

Min, Eungjun. 1999. *Reading the Homeless: The Media's Image of Homeless Culture*. Westport, CT: Praeger.

Min, Eungjun, and Insung Whang. 1999. Discourse analysis of television news on public antagonism against the homeless. In *Reading the Homeless: The Media's Image of Homeless Culture*, ed. E. Min, 95–107. Westport, CT: Praeger.

Minh-ha, Trinh T. 1989. Woman, native, other. Bloomington: Indiana University Press.

———. 1997. Not you/like you: Postcolonial women and the interlocking questions of identity and difference. In *Dangerous Liaisons: Gender, Nation and Postcolonial Perspectives*, eds. A. McClintock, A. Mufti, and E. Shohat, 415–419. Minneapolis: University of Minnesota.

Mitchell, Juliet. 1971. *Woman's Estate*. New York: Pantheon.

———. 1990. Women: The longest revolution. In *Women, Class and the Feminist Imagination: A Socialist-Feminist Reader*, eds. K. Hansen and I. Philipson, 43–73. Philadelphia: Temple University Press.

Moerman, Michael. 1992. Life after C.A.: An ethnographer's autobiography. In *Text in Context: Contributions to Ethnomethodology*, eds. G. Watson and R. Seiler, 20–34. Newbury Park, CA: Sage.

Mohanty, Chandra Talpade. 1985. Under Western eyes: Feminist scholarship and colonial discourses. *Boundary* 3:333–358.

Moloney, Molly, and Sarah Fenstermaker. 2002. Performance and accomplishment: Reconciling feminist conceptions of gender. In *Doing Gender, Doing Difference: Inequality, Power and Institutional Change*, eds. S. Fenstermaker and C. West, 189–216. New York: Routledge.

Moraga, Cherríe, and Gloria Anzuldua. 1983. *This Bridge Called My Back*. New York: Kitchen Table: Women of Color Press.

Moran-Ellis, Jo, Victoria Alexander, Ann Cronin, Mary Dickinson, Jane Fielding, Judith Sleney, and Hilary Thomas. 2006. Triangulation and integration: Processes, claims and implications. *Qualitative Research* 6 (7):45–59.

Morley, David. 2000. Home territories: Media, mobility and identity. New York: Routledge.

Morrison, Toni. 1992. *Race-Ing Justice, En-Gendering Power: Essays on Anita Hill, Clarence Thomas, and the Construction of Social Reality*. New York: Pantheon.

Muñoz, José Esteban. 1998. *Disidentifications: Queers of Color and the Performance of Politics*. Minneapolis: University of Minnesota.

Muraleedharan, T. 2003. Rereading Gandhi. In *Displacing Whiteness*, ed. by R. Frankenberg, 60–85. Durham, NC: Duke University Press.

Museum of Broadcast Communications. 2006. Cable Networks. Retrieved January 5, 2006. http://www.museum.tv/archives/etv/C/htmlC/cablenetwork/cablenetwork.htm

Nash, Suzanne. 1993. *Home and Its Dislocations in Nineteenth Century France*. Albany: State University of New York Press.

National Alliance to End Homelessness. 2002 [cited 2005]. Available from http://www.endhomelessness.org/.

National Committee on Pay Equity. 2005. Research report. The National Committee on Pay Equity. Available from http://www.pay-equity.org/

Nieves, Evelyn. 2005. Fla. tomato pickers still reap "harvest of shame." *Washington Post*, A3, February 28.

Nix, Crystal. 1986. Taking account of the hidden homeless. *New York Times*, E8, June 22.

Nixon, Sean. 1997. Exhibiting masculinity. In *Representation: Cultural Representations and Signifying Practices*, ed. S. Hall, 291–336. Thousand Oaks, CA: Sage.

Norman, Michael. 1983. Indigents moved by city trying to cope in Jersey. *New York Times*, 26L.

O'Hara, Ann, and Emily Cooper. 2003. Priced Out [cited 2005]. Technical Assistance Collaborative, Inc. Available from http://www.tacinc.org

Oakley, Ann. 1972. *Sex, Gender, and Society*. Oxford: Martin Robertson.

Oliver, Myrna. 1984. County sued sgain on shelter for homeless. *Los Angeles Times*, 5.

Omi, Michael. 1996. Racialization in the post-civil rights era. In *Mapping Multi-Culturalism*, eds. A. Gordon and C. Newfield, 178–186. Minneapolis: University of Minnesota Press.

Omi, Michael, and Howard Winant. 1994. *Racial Formation in the United States: From the 1960s to the 1990s*. London: Routledge.

Overend, William. 1983. A time of crisis for our brothers' keepers. *Los Angeles Times*. 1, 2.

Palachunk, O. Marie. 1994. Malicious harassment statutes: A constitutional fight against bias-motivated crime. *Gonzaga Law Review* 29:359–422.

Parsons, Talcott. 1970. *Social Structure and Personality*. New York: The Free Press.

———. 1971. *The System of Modern Societies*, ed. A. Inkeles. Englewood Cliffs NJ: Prentice-Hall.

Parsons, Talcott, and Edward Shils. 1951. *Toward a General Theory of Action*. New York: Harper & Row.

Pascale, Celine-Marie. 1995. *The Public Response to Homelessness*. MA thesis, San José State University, San José, California.

———. 2001. All in a day's work: A feminist analysis of class formation and social identity. *Race, Gender, and Class* 8:34–59.

———. 2005. There's no place like home: The discursive production of homelessness. *Cultural Studies/Critical Methodologies* 5:250–268.

Pascale, Celine-Marie and Candace West. 1997. Social illusions: Responses to homelessness in Santa Cruz, California, 1989–1994. *Perspectives on Social Problems* 9:1–29.

Patai, Daphne. 1991. U.S. academics and third world women: Is ethical research possible? In *Women's Words: The Feminist Practice of Oral History*, eds. S. B. Gluck and D. Patai, 137–158. New York: Routledge.

Pêcheux, Michel. 1982. *Language, Semantics and Ideology*. Trans. H. Nagpal. New York: St. Martin's Press.

———. 1994. The mechanism of ideological (mis)recognition. In *Mapping Ideology*, ed. S. Zizek, 141–151. New York: Verso.

Perkins, Broderick. 1999. $400,000...and rising. *San Jose Mercury News*, A1, A24, May 4.

Perry, Pamela. 2004. Shades of white: *White Kids and Racial Identities in High School*. Durham, NC: Duke University Press.

Perry, Tony. 1994. Spiritual feud over homeless divides city. *Los Angeles Times*, A3, A19, September 26.

Peterson, I. (1983). Warm season masks but doesn't end problem of the homeless. *New York Times*, A16 (L).

Pinsky, Mark. 1985. A new class of homeless on horizon. *Los Angeles Times*, 1, 3, March 27.

Piven, Francis Fox, and Richard Cloward. 1979. *Poor People's Movements: How they Succeed, How They Fail*. New York: Vintage Books.

Pollner, Melvin. 1987. *Mundane Reason: Reality in Everyday and Sociological Discourse*. Cambridge: Cambridge University Press.

Potter, Jonathan. 2004. Discourse analysis. In *Handbook of Data Analysis*, eds. M. Hardy and A. Bryman, 607–624. Thousand Oaks, CA: Sage.

Poulantzas, Nicos. 1975. *Classes in Contemporary Capitalism*. London: NLB.

———. 1982. On social classes. In *Classes, Power, and Conflict: Classical and Contemporary Debates*, eds. A. Giddens and D. Held, 101–111. Berkeley: University of California Press.

Power, Gerald. 1999. Media image and the culture of homelessness: Possibilities for identification. In *Reading the Homeless: The Media's Image of Homeless Culture*, ed. E. Min, 65–83. Westport, CT: Praeger.

Pratt, Mary Louise. 1985. Scratches on the face of the country; or, what Mr. Barrow saw in the land of the bushmen. In *Race, Writing, and Difference*, ed. J. Henry Louis Gates, 138–162. Chicago: University of Chicago.

Przeworski, Adam. 1978. Proletariat into a class: The process of class formation from Karl Kautsky's the class struggle to recent controversies. *Politics and Society* 7 (4):343–401.

———. 1985. *Capitalism and Social Democracy*. Cambridge: Cambridge University Press.

Psathas, George. 1992. The study of extended sequences: The case of the garden lesson. In *Text in Context: Contributions to Ethnomethodology*, eds. G. Watson and R. Seiler, 99–122. Newbury Park, CA: Sage Publications.

Punch, Keith. 2005. *Introduction to Social Research* (2nd ed.). Thousand Oaks, CA: Sage Publications.

Purdy, Matthew. 1994. Homeless sleeping in city office: Last resort is now part of system. *New York Times*, 1, 25, December 12.

Purnick, Joyce. 1985. Police to round up homeless when a cold wave grips city. *New York Times*, A1, B8.

Ragin, Charles, Joan Nagel, and Patricia White. 2003. General guidance for developing qualitative research projects. In *Workshop on Scientific Foundations of Qualitative Research*, eds. C. Ragin, J. Nagel, and P. White, 9–16. Arlington, VA: National Science Foundation.

Reisigl, Martin, and Ruth Wodak. 2001. *Discourse and Discrimination*. New York: Routledge.

Rich, Adrienne. 1980. Compulsorary heterosexuality and lesbian existence. *Signs* 5:631–660.

Rich, Spencer. 1990. Mayors report surge in emergency food, shelter requests. *Washington Post*. A17, December 20.

Rimer, Sara. 1985. At 28, a prologue of promise but a life in rags. *New York Times*, 16, July 18.

Robbins, William. 1983. Welfare cutoff swelling Philadelphia's homeless. *New York Times*. 8N, September 18.

Roediger, David. 1991. *The Wages of Whiteness*. London: Verso.

———. 1994. *Towards the Abolition of Whiteness: Essays on Race, Politics, and Working Class History*. New York: Verso.

———. 2002. *Colored White: Transcending the Racial Past*. Berkeley: University of California Press.

Rose, Vicki McNickle. 1977. Rape as a social problem: A byproduct of the feminist movement. *Social Problems* 25, 75–89.

Rule, Sheila. 1983. Neighbors join to assist shelter on the east side. *New York Times*, 11N.

Sacks, Harvey. 1992. On doing "Being Ordinary." In *Structures of Social Action: Studies in Conversation Analysis*, eds. J. M. Atkinson and J. Heritage, 413–440. Cambridge: Cambridge University Press.

Saukko, Paula. 2003. *Doing Research in Cultural Studies*. Thousand Oaks, CA: Sage.

Saxton, Alexander. 1971. *The Indispensable Enemy: Labor and the Anti-Chinese Movement in California*. Berkeley: University of California Press.

———. 1990. *The Rise and Fall of the White Republic: Class Politics and Mass Culture in Nineteenth-Century America*. New York: Verso.

Schneider, Joseph. 1978. Deviant drinking as disease: Alcoholism as a social accomplishment. *Social Problems* 25:361–372.

———. 1984. Morality, social problems and everyday life. In *Studies in the Sociology of Social Sroblems*, eds. J. Schneider and J. Kitsuse, 180–205. Norwood, NJ: Ablex.

Scott, Joan. 1988. *Gender and the Politics of History*. New York: Columbia University Press.

———. 1991. The evidence of experience. *Critical Inquiry* 17:773–797.

Seed, Patricia. 2001. *American Pentimento: The Invention of Indians and the Pursuit of Riches*. Minneapolis: University of Minnesota Press.

Sedgwick, Eve. 1990. *Epistemology of the Closet*. Berkeley: University of California Press.

Seidman, Steven. 1994. *Contested Knowledge: Social Theory in the Postmodern Era*. Cambridge, MA: Blackwell Publishers.

———. 1997a. *Difference Troubles: Queering Social Theory and Sexual Politics*. Cambridge: Cambridge University Press.

———. 1997b. Relativizing sociology: The challenge of cultural studies. In *From Sociology to Cultural Studies*, eds. E. Long, 37–61. Malden, MA: Backwell.

Shapiro, Judith. 1991. Transsexualism: Reflections on the persistence of gender and the mutability of sex. In *Body Guards: The Cultural Politics of Gender Ambiguity*, eds. J. Epstein and K. Straub, 248–279. New York: Routledge.

Sharrock, Wes, and Bob Anderson. 1986. *The Ethnomethodologists*, ed. P. Hamilton. London: Tavistock Publications.

Shogern, Elizabeth. 1994. Cities seek solutions to dilemma of homelessness. *Los Angeles Times*, A1, February 7.

Siegal, Allan M., and William G. Connolly. 1999. *The New York Times Manual of Style and Usage*. New York: Three Rivers Press.

Silverman, David. 2004. *Interpreting Qualitative Data: Methods for Analyzing Text, Talk and Interaction*. (2nd ed.). Thousand Oaks, CA: Sage (Orig. pub. 1993.)

Smith, David Lionel. 1998. What is black culture? In *The House that Race Built*, ed. W. Lubiano. New York: Vintage.

Smith, Dorothy. 1990a. *The Conceptual Practices of Power*. Boston: Northeastern University Press.

———. 1990b. *Texts, Facts, and Feminity: Exploring the Relations of Ruling*. New York: Routledge.

———. 1999. *Writing the Social: Critique, Theory and Investigations*. Toronto: University of Toronto Press.

Smother, Ronald. 1986. At men's shelter in Beford-Stuyvesant, a room for 532. *New York Times*, B1, B4, November 9.

Spector, Malcolm, and John Kitsuse. 1987. *Constructing Social Problems*. New York: Aldine de Gruyter.

Staff. 1989. Shelter for homeless will open. *Los Angeles Times*. A31, December 30.

———. 1990. City-run camps for homeless studied. *Los Angeles Times*, A35, November 24.

———. 1995. Bar patron tied to one-third of new Minneapolis TB cases. *Los Angeles Times*, B2, June 27.

Stein, Mark. 1986. Silicon Valley's homeless aren't jobless—they just don't earn enough. *Los Angeles Times*, 23, October 5.

Stoler, Ann Laura. 1995. *Race and the Education of Desire: Foucault's History of Sexuality and the Colonial Order of Things*. Durham, NC: Duke University Press.

Stoller, Robert. 1968. *Sex and Gender*. New York: J. Aronson.

Stone, Sandy. 1998. The empire strikes back: A posttransexual manifesto. In *The Visible Woman: Imaging Technologies, Gender, and Science*, eds. P. Treichler, L. Cartwright, and C. Penley, 285–307. New York: New York University Press.

Sullivan, Joseph. 1983. The homeless: Officials differ on the causes. *New York Times*. B9L, November 24.

———. 1988. Homeless families create a community. *New York Times*. 29, 30.

Sumrall, Amber Coverdale. 1992. *Write to the Heart: Wit and Wisdom of Women Writers*. Freedom, CA: Crossings Press.

Terry, Don. 1995. In Chicago, a homeless man gains currency in death. *New York Times*. 9, September 10.

Threadgold, Terry. 1997. *Feminist Poetics: Poiesis, Performance, Histories*. New York: Routledge.

Todorov, Tzvetan. 1995. *The Morals of History*. Trans. A. Waters. Minneapolis: University of Minnesota Press.

Toth, Jennifer. 1991. Number of children living on America's streets swells. *Los Angeles Times*, A5, October 31.

Trask, Haunani-Kay. 1993. *From a Native Daughter: Colonialism and Sovereignty in Hawaii*. Monroe, ME: Common Courage.

United Press International. 1992. *UPI Stylebook: The Authoritative Handbook for Writers, Editors & News Directors*. Lincolnwood, IL: National Textbook Company.

Van Dijik, Teun A. 1993. Principles of discourse analysis. *Discourse and Society* 4:249–83.

———. 1997. *Discourse as Social Interaction*. London: Sage.

Vidal-Ortiz, Salvador. 2004. On being a white person of color. *Qualitative Sociology* 27 (2):197–203.

Volosinov, V. N. 1973. *Marxism and the Philosophy of Language*. Trans. L. Matejka and I. R. Titunik. Cambdrige, MA: Harvard University Press.

Walker, Jill. 1989. Brother, can you spare a coupon? *Washington Post*, A3.

Walker, Margaret Urban. 1998. *Moral Understandings: A Feminist Study in Ethics*. New York: Routledge.

Ware, Vron. 1992. *Beyond the Pale: White Women, Racism, and History*. New York: Verso.

Watkins, Evan. 1998. *Everyday Exchanges: Marketwork and Capitalist Common Sense*. Stanford, CA: Stanford University Press.

Watson, Graham, and Robert Seiler. 1992. *Text in Context: Contributions to Ethnomethodology*. Newbury Park, CA: Sage Publications.

Webb, Robert A. 1978. The *Washington Post Deskbook on Style*. San Francisco: McGraw-Hill Book Company.

Weber, Max. 1978. *Economy and Society: An Outline of Interpretive Sociology*, (vols. 1 & 2). eds. G. Roth and C. Wittich, trans. H. G. Ephraim Fischoff, A. M. Henderson, Ferdinand Kolegar, C. Wright Mills, Talcott Parsons, Max Rheinstein, Guenther Roth, Edward Shils, and Claus Wittich. Berkeley: University of California Press.

———. 1995. *General Economic History*. Trans. F. H. Knight. New Brunswick, NJ: Transaction Publishers.

Weiss, Gilbert, and Ruth Wodak. 2003. *Critical Discourse Analysis*. New York: Palgrave MacMillan.

Wellman, David. 1993. *Portraits of White Racism*. Cambridge: Cambridge University Press.

West, Candace, and Sarah Fenstermaker. 1995a. Doing difference. *Gender and Society* 9:8–37.

———. 1995b. Reply: (Re)doing difference. *Gender and Society* 9:506–513.

———. 1999. Accountability in action: The accomplishment of gender, race, and class in a meeting of the University of California Board of Regents, 1–48. (Unpublished manuscript.)

West, Candace, and Don Zimmerman. 1977. Women's place in everyday talk: Reflections on parent-child interactions. *Social Problems* 24:521–529.

West, Candace, and Don H. Zimmerman. 1987. Doing gender. *Gender and Society* 1:125–151.

Wetherell, Margaret, and Jonathan Potter. 1987. *Discourse and Social Psychology*. Thousand Oaks, CA: Sage Publications.

Wetherell, Margaret. 1998. Positioning and interpretative repertoires: Conversation analysis and poststructuralism in dialog. *Discourse and Society* 9:387–412.

Wetherell, Margaret, Stephanie Taylor, and Simeon Yates. 2001. *Discourse Theory and Practice*. London: Sage.

Williams, Frank. 1994. Setting up homeless camp has its skeptics. *Los Angeles Times*, B1, B8, October 15.

Williams, Glyn. 1999. *French Discourse Analysis: The Method of Post-Structuralism*. New York: Routledge.

Williams, Juan. 1984. Homeless choose to be, Reagan says. *Washington Post*, A1, A4, February 1.

Wilton, Tamsin. 1996. Which one is the man? The heterosexualization of of lesbian sex. In *Theorizing Heterosexuality: Telling it Straight*, ed. D. Richardson, 75–90. Buckingham: Open University Press.

Wittgenstein, Ludwig. 1951. *Philosophical Investigations*. Trans. G. E. M. Anscombe. New York: Macmillan.

Wodak, Ruth. 2001. What CDA is about—a summary of its history, important concepts and developments. In *Methods of Critical Discourse Analysis*, eds. R. Wodak and M. Meyer, 1–13. Thousand Oaks, CA: Sage.

Wodak, Ruth, Rudolf de Cillia, Martin Reisigl, and Karin Liebhart. 1999. *The Discursive Construction of National Identity.* Trans. A. Hirsch and R. Mitten. Edinburgh: Edinburgh University Press.

Wood, Linda A., and Rolf Kroger. 2000. *Doing Discourse Analysis: Methods for Studying Action in Talk and Text.* Thousand Oaks, CA: Sage.

Wooffitt, Robin. 2005. *Conversation Analysis and Discourse Analysis.* Thousand Oaks, CA: Sage.

Woolgar, Steve, and Dorothy Pawluch. 1985. Ontological gerrymandering. *Social Problems* 32:214–227.

Wright, Erik Olin. 1989. *A General Framework for the Analysis of Class Structure. The Debate on Classes,* ed. E. O. Wright, 3–47. London: Verso.

———. 1997. *Class Counts: Comparative Studies in Class Analysis.* Cambridge: Cambridge University Press.

Wright, Michelle. 2004. *Becoming Black: Creating Identity in the African Diaspora.* Durham, NC: Duke University Press.

Yudice, George. 2003. *The Expediency of Culture.* Durham, NC: Duke University Press.

Zimmerman, Don. 1992. Achieving context: Openings in emergency calls. In *Text in Context: Contributions to Ethnomethodology,* eds. G. Watson and R. Seiler, 35–51. Newbury Park, CA: Sage.

Zinn, Maxine Baca. 1979. Field research in minority communities: Ethical, methodological and political observations by an insider. *Social Problems* 27:209–218.

Zizek, Slavoj. 1994. Introduction. In *Mapping Ideology,* ed. S. Zizek, 1–33. New York: Verso.

INDEX